THE ROAD TO ACCEPTANCE

A Journey of Spiritual Healing

By Caroline L.M. Clark

All Scriptures used are from the King James Version.

Writing Career Coach Press (a division of Writing Career Coach, 14665 Fike Rd., Riga, MI 49276) functions only as book publisher. As such, the ultimate design, content, editorial accuracy, and views expressed or implied in this work are those of the author.

Cover design by Zakr Studio www.zakrstudio.com

ISBN-10 0983360758
ISBN-13 9780983360759

Testimonies from other Raggedys...

I want to give a short sweet testimony Caroline. You can share my name too if you want to.

I met Caroline and the Raggedy group shortly after my husband was diagnosed with pulmonary fibrosis. I felt lost and was unable to communicate clearly with people for awhile, even my writing skills seem to have plummeted. I struggled to stay positive for Jim's sake and then I found this group. I was suffering from being left out of things at church and friends, even Christians seemed to take a step back as if this were a disease they could catch. I was dealing with being in remission of Lupus so Jim and I were somewhat isolated.

The Raggedy Group accept and love Jim and I where we are at. They have spent hours praying for and encouraging me. They've constantly interceded for Jim and I'm happy to say as of today, he has beaten the odds and has lived beyond the time-line given to him. He is fairly strong and one of then things given to him by the group is a sense of his God given purpose. He is a strong prayer warrior and every morning we spend time together in the Word and then pray for the prayer requests that come down in this group. They are powerful and sincere and many answers for all of us come as a result.

We know we are on The Road to Acceptance and love walking with this loving group of God-fearing Christians. Thank you Caroline and all of you for loving and accepting us as Brothers and Sisters in Christ.

Caroline, I write this with great emotion and am crying. Please feel free to take this and use it for God's glory. I have no problem with it being edited to fit your needs. I'm sure there are mistakes because I'm emotional because I love you and you guys have so stuck with us through thick and thin and I can't see for the tears and my thumb hurts! :) The second is that you have reached one of your dreams and I can't wait to read your book. Let me know or your publisher if you need a reviewer or influence r. Congrats Caroline...I'm so Happy Dancing for You!

Blessings,
our Paulette Harris
www.pauletteharris.biz
http://comeandsitawhile.blogspot.com

~~~

My bout with pancreatic cancer started with the statement that 85% of those with my disease die within twelve months. This happy news from the doctor that was checking my X-ray for a kidney stone. The good news, early detection. Prayers by the Raggedys and others were begun.

There were no doctors with necessary experience that would accept my health insurance, a Medicare advantage plan. The big hospitals also rejected the coverage and wouldn't even accept cash. One local surgeon said he had done four similar operations in the past twenty years, but these patients didn't have my problem and he was reluctant. I told my family that, "dying isn't all that bad for a Christian. I was at peace, they weren't. We prayed.

Another local doctor that we had called thought enough about my problem to call back and say the best surgeon was at a Tampa hospital; indeed the only doctor he would have operate if it were him. The Tampa doctor said he would meet with me and worry about insurance later. I was able to change to Medicare and the costs were covered. The doctor said the cancer was operable, many aren't. We prayed!

The day before my operation, a friend called (a Gideon) and said that God had awakened him in the middle of the night. He didn't know why, but got up and prayed. God told him to tell me not to worry; He had me covered for this problem. My friend said, "Bill, God doesn't talk to me every day -wow!" We prayed together.

My Sunday school teachers and classmates met us in Tampa at 6:30 am as we entered the hospital. We prayed! The operation removed one-third of my pancreas, my spleen and my gall bladder. The good news, the operation was successful, the cancer was isolated and it was one of very few that is a slow growing variety. Praise God!

I ended up with the best surgeon in hundreds of miles and in the best hospital. I was cancer free. My bills (low six figures) were 100% paid by Medicare and my supplemental insurance. How did this happen? How such miracles?

Remember David, the little guy that beat the odds?

His Psalm 118 offers an explanation:

5 When hard pressed, I cried to the LORD;
  he brought me into a spacious place.
        ****

14 The LORD is my strength and my defense;
   he has become my salvation.
        ****

16 The LORD's right hand is lifted high;
   the LORD's right hand has done mighty things!"
17 I will not die but live,
   and will proclaim what the LORD has done.
18 The LORD has chastened me severely,
   but he has not given me over to death.
        ****

21 I will give you thanks, for you answered me;
   you have become my salvation.
        ****

23 the LORD has done this,
   and it is marvelous in our eyes.
24 The LORD has done it this very day;
   let us rejoice today and be glad.

My thanks to God, the Raggedys and all the other prayer warriors, known and unknown, who brought me through this. I am a three-year survivor. Is this an awesome God? Praise be to God!!!

our Bill Twomey, member of the Raggedys

About the Author

I began life looking for acceptance.

I can remember my father telling me about how I screamed from my crib because I wanted attention.

I can also remember screaming from my bed during the night. I was terrified of what the night would bring. I desperately wanted the safety of my mother and father. My search for safety and acceptance didn't end until I was 55 years old. I now know that I am safe. I now know that I am accepted by God. I am unique, but I am also like everyone else.

I finished high school when I was 49 years old. I was never strong enough, confident enough in myself, to finish before that time because I believed I was too slow mentally to learn. It was only when my husband and children encouraged—no, pushed— me to go back to school that I tried.

I didn't want to disappoint them.

I received my G.E.D. in three weeks, and then enrolled in a community college. I majored in human services with an emphasis on alcohol and drug counseling. Things went better than I had hoped. I was inducted in national honor societies and received scholarships for my grades. After two years, I transferred to a university and pursued a degree in psychology. Again, I earned awards and recognition for my grades.

I earned my degree in three years, then my master's degree two years later.

In 1978, at the age of 35, I began working in the ministry in Oregon after attending Bible School at my local church. In 1986, six months after my mother went home to the Lord, I moved to Hawaii and had a street outreach ministry where many were saved and delivered from prostitution, alcohol and drugs, and homelessness. While in Hawaii, I was ordained. I returned to Oregon in 1990, and then moved to Oklahoma in 1997 for graduate school at the University of Oklahoma. I was also working for a tribal agency as an alcohol and drug counselor.

We moved to North Carolina, my husband's birthplace, in 2000. I have worked in ministry since that time, including doing HIV testing and counseling, and working as a mental health counselor. One of my passions is public speaking; it still surprises me that I have spoken at universities, colleges, schools, churches, and senior groups and to physicians and nurses.

Acknowledgments

I would like to thank the following people who were "angels" while I wrote this book. Many contributed on a scholarly level, and others contributed by blessing my life.

I could not have written this book without the encouragement of my husband, Sanford; our children, Sabrina, Sanford II (Michael), and DeAnna; and our grandsons, Scott and Micah. They encourage me and bless my life daily. They lift me spiritually and bring laughter to my life.

Neither could I have begun this book without my friends who have become true family—Georgia Jackson (home with the Lord) and her children, Pamela and Denise and all of her grandchildren; especially Natalie and Jessi, also my sisters in the Lord, Teresa Cellura; and Jacqueline Clayton.

There are also angels God has sent me whom I have never met: Reverend Thomas Lacy of Richmond, Virginia; John Lehmann of Virginia, who has become my "little brother" throughout this. I hope one day to meet all of them.

One individual in particular was instrumental in giving me the courage to write this book—Earl Coleman of Thomasville, North Carolina. He first told me, "When you let go of your past, your past lets go of you."

I could not have begun or accomplished this book without the advice and help of Tiffany Colter, my agent, instructor, publisher and friend at WritingCareerCoach.com or Anthony Antenucci of ZAKR Studio, my website designer and printer, a very patient and kind man.

Bless each of you for the prayers, caring, love, and time that you have invested into my life and my spirit. I would not have been me without all of you.

Introduction

Today, I know I have overcome my past. I have a bachelor's degree and a master's degree, but what makes me truly successful is that I am a child of the King, ordained by God from time's beginning.

There was a time when I thought there was no good thing in me. It is what I thought until I was about 40 years old. God had me look in the mirror one morning—I mean, really look. I looked into the pupils in the middle of my eyes and searched deep into my soul.

I didn't want to do it.

It scared me.

I was afraid of what I would see.

I thought I would see demons. I tried to pull away.

But God wouldn't let me.

He made me continue. It seemed like forever—but was probably about twenty or thirty minutes—when I saw something that surprised and even shocked me. There was a beautiful child of God deep within. She was nice. It was the first time the popular saying, "God doesn't make junk," was truly revealed to me.

I was beautiful in His eyes.

This was who He originally created me to be. I liked that person within me. I loved that person and wanted her to come out. I desperately wanted to be her friend. I just never knew she was there.

God showed me that fear, unforgiveness, and events—holding the ugly sin of hatred within—had kept that child in a prison. God was trying to free her for His ultimate purpose, and I was keeping her in literal chains. I thought that I was filled with ugliness and didn't know that there was this creation of God within me. That was such a magnificent revelation to me that I don't think I've ever kept my mouth shut since.

Today, I can look in the mirror and like the chubby older woman peering back at me. It surprises me that I see the same person I have always been, but with a new love for the person in the mirror. The shame I carried is gone! I can see into the heart deep within me, which our precious Lord created, and know I am accepted and loved by my Creator. Too many years were spent trying to run from the only body and spirit our Lord had given me. I always felt that I was slow and ugly. I have always been an observer of others. I notice so many men and women with their heads hung in shame. Those were the people who never walked tall and erect. They didn't want to be noticed or stand out. My heart always went out to them in prayer. I could relate to them. Often I noticed those who were overly confident and I knew they were trying to hide their own insecurities.

I was raised in a family where I was never considered good enough. I was less than the males, and it made a difference in how I lived my life. I tried to destroy myself with drugs and alcohol and all of the negative things that usually go with it. It was an acceptable attempt at suicide, and I believed I could manage it. Who could really blame me if I accidentally overdosed or had an auto accident that would take my life? I believed that perhaps then, my family would have loved me. I would have finally done something well enough.

When I was 27 years old, a very dear friend and a Messianic Jew, Jeanie, told me to stop what I was doing to myself and to the One who created me. Everyone else had told me to stop but never gave me a good enough reason. Everyone else said I was shaming them. I didn't think there was anything abnormal about that. I had already shamed them enough by being born.

No one had ever said that I might be hurting God's heart by what I was doing. How could I, unworthy as I was, possibly hurt God's heart? Did that mean He cared for me?

I couldn't believe that at first. Then Jeanie said to me, "I love you, but I cannot continue to watch you kill yourself. When you're done destroying yourself, call me and I will be here for you."

I stopped using alcohol and drugs that week.

I was in the midst of drinking and my four-year-old son wanted me to play with him. I asked him to leave me alone. He continued pleading with me to play with him, like all children do. In my drunken state I reached over and slapped him across the face. The expression on his face was shock and disbelief. That was my bottom. I could harm myself and it never bothered me, but physically hurting one of my children was a wakeup call. I walked into my front room, sat in a chair, and immediately stopped my drinking and drugging. My children were innocent; how could I hurt them the way I had always been hurt?

I cried to God, I pleaded with Him to deliver me from my lifestyle, I begged my son to forgive me. I held him in my arms as he sobbed and kept telling me how sorry he was he had bothered me. It was also in that moment that God made Himself known to me. I saw the presence of God in the face of my four-year-old son. An awareness of His unconditional love flooded through me and has never left. It has been a long struggle to come to the point where I could say, "Yes, I love myself because I am God's child and I can see His Spirit, His love, His caring, His kindness in my lowly spirit." How miraculous!

But it didn't happen overnight. My love for Him happened instantly when I opened my heart to Him, but my love for myself took much more work.

Contents

Chapter 1
He Is Everywhere

Psalm 139:1-14

O LORD, thou hast searched me, and known me. Thou knowest my downsitting and mine uprising, thou understandest my thought afar off. Thou compassest my path and my lying down, and art acquainted with all my ways. For there is not a word in my tongue, but, lo, O Lord, thou knowest it altogether. Thou hast beset me behind and before, and laid thine hand upon me. Such knowledge is too wonderful for me; it is high, I cannot attain unto it. Whither shall I go from thy spirit? Or whither shall I flee from thy presence? If I ascend up into heaven, thou art there: if I make my bed in hell, behold thou art there. If I take the wings of the morning, and dwell in the uttermost parts of the sea; Even there shall thy hand lead me, and thy right hand shall hold me. If I say, Surely the darkness shall cover me; even the night shall be light about me. Yea, the darkness hideth not from thee; but the night shineth as the day: the darkness and the light are both alike to thee. For thou hast possessed my reins: thou hast covered me in my mother's womb. I will praise thee; for I am fearfully and wonderfully made: marvelous are thy works: and that my soul knoweth right well.

Now faith is the substance of things hoped for, the evidence of things not seen (Hebrews 11:1).

Therefore, if any man be in Christ, he is a new creature: old things are passed away; behold, all things are become new (2 Corinthians 5:17).

How often have we wished, prayed, pleaded, and begged for a healing from our past? We are the total of every moment we have lived. Because we are earthly creatures, and because of the wonderful manner in which our God has designed our brain, filling it with memory, we have retained the good and the bad in our lives. Our minds have been the most marvelous recording devices ever created. This is wonderful when it comes to remembering our good and happy times, the times we have learned new things. Our minds can also hinder us when we remember and chose to dwell on the negative experiences. When we dwell on the negative and hurtful things in our lives those are the times they tear us down, we need to pray and praise our Lord until the thoughts are gone. Dwelling on the negative never helped me and will never help anyone else. Keep mind busy with positive things.

Now in times of stress, I close my eyes for a second and remember the smell of the crisp, clean mountain air in Oregon. I used to sit on a rock or a log and look up at the mighty trees and brilliant blue sky that our God created.

Other times I would enjoy the rare sighting of a strong buck or the graceful lines of a doe, ever watchful of her fawn.

Still other times, I remember the magnificent warmth and colors of the Pacific Ocean off the coast of Kailua Beach in Hawaii, from aqua at its shallowest to the blues and purples of the deeper waters as I walked the beach every morning. Those memories are embedded in my hardware. Those memories aid in healing during stressful times.

There are other memories that are just as clear and sharp: being called names like "a waste of time" when I was a child. I remember abuse, punishments (whether rightfully deserved or not), and being looked upon as learning disabled by the nuns at the school I attended. The absolute worst thing was being a girl. My grandmother had nine children, all married with children of their own. We lived upstairs of my grandmother, grandfather, and uncle.

There was a three-bedroom flat on the bottom where my grandparents lived and a three-bedroom flat upstairs where we lived. The doors were never locked. The relatives would come and go at will, especially when my grandmother was cooking her wonderful Lebanese food. My mother's brother lived downstairs from us and my mother's sister would come every day to babysit my brother and me and help my grandmother.

My mother's brothers and one of her sisters considered me to be less than worthy. I can still vividly recall the many times I would spontaneously vomit on my desk at school, due to the stresses in my home life. That would be followed by the horrible stares from the other young students as they backed away from me so as to avoid the illness themselves.

It was a time when I had no control. It was a time when other students were fearful of my malady and found it hard to accept me. They were children. It was also a time when I first came to believe that no one cared for me, not even God.

I can still remember stories told of me lying in my bed and screaming from fear. The fear was of the darkness and the shadows that surrounded me. Fear of being hurt, of being in pain, was all too real to me from my earliest memories.

My mother's family was from Lebanon, and most of them had come to America from Beirut. My maternal grandmother was wonderful, but I could never understand what happened to the rest of my mother's family; they were always filled with anger and rage.

The families of other children I knew appeared happy. I didn't understand why mine was different. Although my mother and father gave me unconditional love, I didn't understand why the rest of the family didn't.

Their abusive words and actions toward me had to have been my fault. I couldn't create any other explanation. The abuse I endured from my aunt, uncle, and brother helped to reinforce my confusion and the belief that everything that was wrong was my fault.

My aunt used to tell me that I should have been thrown from a cliff when I was born. I would watch my grandmother show such an abundance of love to everyone, but I only experienced hatred from my aunt and uncle. I never understood that it wasn't me they hated, it was my gender.

My grandfather, although loving to me, was an alcoholic. He and my uncle, his stepson, would occasionally get into fist fights when they were drunk. I remember my grandfather bringing out his pearl-handled gun and threatening to kill my uncle. It seemed someone was always fighting, and my grandmother would get in the middle and try to make peace between them.

One notable day I came in from school and found my grandmother's normally neat kitchen a disaster. My grandfather was lying on the floor with the tall freestanding white metal kitchen cabinet on top of him and dishes and cups broken everywhere. I called to my grandmother and ran through the house looking for her but couldn't find her. I was so afraid that my grandfather was dead. My uncle was passed out on his bed with blood all over his face, his gun lying on the bed. I just knew they were both dead. Absolute terror filled me.

I ran to the kitchen and fell on my knees beside my grandfather begging him to wake up. My grandmother came in through the back door with a look of disbelief and utter sadness. She had walked over a mile to the grocery store and over a mile back and had no idea that they both had gotten drunk once again.

She grabbed me immediately and began hugging me and telling me that they were just playing a game and must have fallen. I knew better. I knew they hated each other. I also knew they were both drunks, but I tried to make them love me, accept me. I always tried to be quiet, polite, and obedient. Whatever was asked of me, I did. I thought if I could be good enough, they wouldn't fight, since I *knew* all of it was my fault.

I believe that my grandfather loved me to the best of his ability to love anyone. He used to take me with him when he walked to the bar and paid me a nickel not to tell my grandmother where he had been. When we returned home, my grandmother would pay me a nickel to tell her if he had been drinking.

I didn't want to lie to my grandmother but I didn't want her and my grandfather to argue, either. If I didn't see him drinking, I could safely say that I didn't see him doing it. So as soon as my grandfather and I would get to the bar, I would tell him that I had to go to the restroom. I would go in there and stay until I thought he was about done drinking and then I would come out. He was usually just paying his bill.

I do not believe my uncle loved me. I don't know if he hated me so deeply because his children were taken away from him by his wife during a divorce, or if there was another reason. I only know that I was never good enough.

That was the atmosphere I was reared in. This was the beginning of my search for a God who loved me and accepted *me*—a female, sins and flaws and all.

Summary and Reflection
Read Psalms 1 and Proverbs 1

I didn't know what it was to have love and comfort when I was growing up, except from my mother, father, and grandmother. This had an influence on how I perceived God and his love for me.

Whether you had a wonderful upbringing or a difficult one, others have also influenced your perception of God.

1.   Consider your upbringing, experiences, and self-perception (both good and bad). How do these influence the way you see God? Is He a pushover? A ruthless dictator? An unwavering judge? A loving comforter?

2.   Do you accept that there is untapped potential within yourself? Don't answer too quickly. If someone asked you to do something you've never done before without giving much direction, what would be your response? That is an indication of how you truly view yourself.

3.   Think of your three greatest challenges currently. These are the things that consume your thoughts. Now think of the three greatest victories you've experienced with God. Find scriptures for each of these (yes, a total of six scriptures). You want scriptures that show what God's Word is in each of these situations.

4.   Take those six scriptures above and meditate on them this way. Read them and then take a moment to envision what your life would look like if what they said was really true. For example, Jude 24 says, "To Him [Jesus] who is able to keep you from falling and to present you before His glorious presence without fault and with great joy." What would your life look like if Jesus could keep you

from falling? Would you trust Him more? Or what if Psalm 89:34 were true: *My covenant will I not break, nor alter the thing that is gone out of my lips.* What if you really believed God could not lie? Envision your life full of the promises of God.

Of course, these Words are true! Go out and look at how you see God and why. Then dig into His word and see who He really is, and meditate each day on that. Let it begin to change who you are from the inside out.

Chapter 2
The Gift

Hebrews 11:1 says: *Now faith is the substance of things hoped for, the evidence of things not seen.* What God was trying to tell His children was that we have something; that His love and acceptance is there for us, within our grasp, even though we cannot see the love He freely gives. We are told to look to God for the answer to our prayer of restoration to Him, to our families, to our friends, to humanity, and we pray, plead and beg: "Make me worthy, make me the same as everyone else, make them love me, make me as good and acceptable as everyone else."

We plod through our days and nights, building up the negatives that a few have dropped into our lives and we hold onto those things and believe them. Our lives are formed from those negatives, ignoring all the positives that God has placed in our lives. Who keeps all those negatives in our minds? Is it satan's trick? Often we haven't yet given ourselves completely to the Lord, we hold on to the negative. Satan is good at helping us to keep these negative thoughts.

In Hebrews 11:1 (paraphrased), it reads that faith is the substance of things hoped for, it is the essence, the beginning, the stuff, the material that God has given us. It says that faith in all things wonderful, holy and pure is there, waiting for us to take it, claim it, and make it a part of ourselves and our being. It's been there all along! We look the other way and search, never finding the substance. It's as though we are children at Christmas, looking everywhere for presents that we know are there, but we can't seem to find. We may find a box that's been wrapped in beautiful paper and ribbon, but we're afraid to shake it too hard or attempt to take a peek. We're afraid to tear the paper.

But God has created this beautiful gift, this substance, and says to us "Tear it open! It's yours! Take it and use it to bless your life!"

We're afraid, so we never open it. We back away, for fear of being caught. And we never experience the beauty of what is inside. The forgiveness, the worthiness, the all-encompassing love and acceptance remains unused. We want to fully give ourselves to God, but we try to hold on to something that isn't God. Many of us go through our entire lives and never look at what's inside that precious box. I think we are afraid we will be disappointed.

Often we say we haven't been blessed with the faith of others. In Acts 10:34, the scripture tells us that God is not a respecter of persons. He never looks on one more highly than another. We look at those who are confident, successful, and happy and assume they have greater faith than we do. Faith is not something that we are able to get or grow on our own. God has blessed us with it from the beginning. It's a form of anticipatory grace. Children have an unquestioning faith. We simply need to believe it and stand in it. Become His child again!

Unfaithfulness is what is taught to us by society. Faith is already there, from the beginning of time. *For I say, through the grace given unto me, to every man that is among you, not to think [of himself] more highly than he ought to think; but to think soberly, according as God hath dealt to every man the measure of faith* (Romans 12:3). God has given us our faith. It is nothing that we have to work for or earn. It is there. God is telling us in this scripture that what we have sincerely looked for is waiting for us to take hold of it.

Often, we feel that others have a great faith, but none of us knows what is going on inside of them. They may be filled with insecurities or phobias of every kind.

They may also be on their knees more than we are, praying for God to help them through every moment of every day. They may have truly surrendered completely to God through all the bad and good.

Someone told me a while ago that I seemed to have a lot of faith. I said, "Yes, I do have a lot of faith. I have faith that God is a God of order." He's holding the universe together. If He was not holding it together, everything would be tumbling down on us. **But I have no faith apart from God.** It is just my believing that what God says is true. I never doubt Him or what He says. It's *me* I doubt. I have insecurities, as we all do.

One of my insecurities is shopping malls. I hate shopping malls because I become claustrophobic. I hate shopping in large stores, really any store, because of it. My brother used to force me into a dark closet while holding it closed when I was young and refuse to let me out. I have disliked being confined in any space since then.

Faith in myself doesn't get me into a shopping mall when I have to go. It is my faith in God. I know that what God says, He means. *In all thy ways acknowledge Him, and he shall direct thy paths* (Proverbs 3:6). If I'm in a mall today, it's because He directs my steps while I am there, and I know He will take care of me. I no longer hyperventilate or become filled with fear being in a confined space. We all have those things that trouble us, worry us, and frighten us.

Becoming a Christian and trusting in the Lord doesn't make us superhuman or robotic. It just makes us God's kids. We are still just little kids, raggedy kids, no matter our age.

I have often heard that the quickest solution to every problem is how long it takes us to get from a standing position to our knees. I do not believe that we actually have to fall to our knees to pray to our Father. We can pray anywhere and at any time. I often pray as I'm walking from meeting to meeting during the day. Often while I'm driving, I'm also talking to God. And often, I have to admit, when others are speaking to me, I slip into a few seconds of prayer.

Prayer is nothing more than communication with God, our Creator, our best Friend. He knows our inside and outside. He knows the beginning and end of each of us. *For the eyes of the Lord run to and fro throughout the whole earth, to shew himself strong in the behalf of them whose heart is perfect toward him. Herein thou hast done foolishly: therefore from henceforth thou shalt have wars* (2 Chronicles 16:9). There is nothing we can hide from Him.

Many times when I'm in a situation, I say to Him, "I'm feeling really ugly right now, God. I want to just say something really nasty to this person and I need your help right now. Help me to silence my mouth and my thoughts and bring them into focus with your thoughts and your will."

After praying that to my Father, I am forced to keep my mouth shut—although sometimes I still blow it. After a while, sometimes a long while, I get in tune with God's will and I can see the other person's views. I may not always agree with them, but at least I can understand them better.

It is usually another person's perceptions of us or our actions that bother us. A perception is simply the way *we* see something.

It is not always factual.

We do not have to respond negatively, and often we do not even have to respond positively.

But we do have to give the person respect as creations of our Heavenly Father. It makes no difference if they are believers or not. None of us knows the future of our own lives, much less another's. We have no idea if God's perfect and ultimate plan is to bring them to a position of greatness. We may have planted the beginning of a small seed of God's will in their life. "*Not as I will, but as thou wilt* (Matthew 26:39b).

I might know that another has done something wrong, but I don't know what circumstances or events led that person to the point of whatever they have chosen to do. I may have made the same choice or same mistake if I had led that person's life. William J. Toms said, "Be careful how you live. You may be the only Bible some person ever reads." That means that we need to not only walk in integrity, but our actions must also model a life that honors God and His Word.

Praise Him that He is your Father, your All; that He chose to create this beautiful orderly world. Praise Him for the stars and the universe, for the wind that blows to refresh us, for the trees and the flowers, for the mighty oceans and rivers, and for the calm, still lakes. There is no end to what He should be praised for. Praise Him for the forgiveness you have because of His Son, Jesus Christ. Praise Him for salvation and for directing your steps. Praise Him that you have the ability to read this right now.

There is also a time to get on your knees and weep before Him. When you or a loved one is ill, or when the cares of this world are just too much to bear, get before Him and cry to Him. He is a Father who hears His children. He is always there to listen and comfort. He is always there to answer. The answer may not always be what you want, but rest assured that He will do what is best, not just for you, but for the overall good of the world.

One time when I was young, I asked my father why it didn't stop raining when I prayed and asked God to make it stop so that I could do something I had planned. My Dad said, "Honey, what if there was a farmer praying for God to keep the rains coming so that his crops could grow? What if no rain meant the farmer's crops would die and the farmer would go broke and lose his farm? God considers everyone's prayers and works for the best for all."

I've never forgotten that wisdom and have repeated it to my own children and grandchildren many times over the years. We must be content with what God gives us. Not just content, but we must praise Him for what He permits to come into our lives. We don't know the reasons behind what God has permitted. Often it's to mature us and often it's to be a witness to another person. I don't always know or discern the reasons for anything. I just try to praise Him through all things.

That's not to say that I always do that. Many times I have to grumble and stumble and have a little pity party for myself, and then I give it up and say, "Not my will but Thine be done." The one thing that I know for sure is that God will never leave us nor forsake us, even if a situation arises when it feels that way. I know that He is a Father who loves us so much that He gave the life of His only Son to die for each of us (John 3:16). We then can stand before the Father, and it's not us He sees any longer. He cannot see the sin we've repented of. All He can see is the blood of His precious Son, Jesus Christ.

Summary and Reflection

Read Psalms 2 and Proverbs 2

Faith is the evidence of what we don't see. God uses our faith to work His will in the earth and Faith is what gives us the hope we need to push through difficult times. It is that hope, born of faith, that will refresh us when everything around us tells us to give up.

1. Consider how your words or actions may have impacted another (whether positively or negatively). Spend time in prayer asking God to help your actions in every situation to conform to His will.
2. Practice ways to hold your tongue. When there is a situation that causes you to "feel ugly" on the inside, whisper a prayer and ask God to help you to handle the situation. Then just shut up.
3. Spend time reflecting on all you have to be thankful for. Write a praise report out where you list things, little and big, that God has done to bless you, protect, provide for, or teach.

Finally, go to Hebrews 11 and read what it says about faith. Meditate on these words and consider how your own faith walk is maturing.

Chapter 3
Witnessing

While living in Hawaii, I kept a prayer journal. I lived there for about four years and had a street ministry in Honolulu. I would go down to where I ministered about 9 in the evening and stay out there until about 4 or 5 in the morning. God has always called me to minister to the underprivileged, the prostitutes, the addicts, the alcoholics and the homeless. I loved my ministry more than anything I have ever done in my life. I have never been a night person, but I came alive while I was on the streets ministering to them.

When I say I ministered to them, I do not mean that I was there to preach hellfire and damnation. God sent me there to love them just as they were. There were many who got into treatment for their addictions, and many accepted Jesus as their Lord and Savior. They became my friends. I sat on the curb with them and we talked. Often, God gave me something to share with them that there was no way I could have known unless the Holy Spirit revealed it to me. It was a witness for them and for me.

One time I asked a man sitting on the curb if I could talk about Jesus with him. He said, "Buy me a beer and I'll listen to anything you have to say." I began to walk away, but the Holy Spirit convicted my heart to buy him a beer and tell him how much God loves him. I was shocked and wondered how my pastor would react when I shared this with him.

However, I did go to the closest store and bought him a beer. I gave him the beer and told him how much God loved him. We talked for a long time on the curb that night. As I was leaving that morning to return home and get some sleep, the man came back to me and asked if I could help him get into treatment. I was elated. I knew that the Lord had truly spoken to me.

I knew there was a Christian organization on Maui that helped people and I arranged to have the gentleman go there. After some time I moved back to the mainland and began going to the University in Oregon. One day, I was walking across campus and a nice-looking man was walking almost into me. I moved and he moved.

Finally he said, "You don't remember me, do you?"

No, I didn't.

He told me the story of our meeting in Hawaii and how successful he was with the alcohol treatment, and he thanked me for listening to God, buying him the beer that night, and helping him. I told him it sure wasn't me, because in the flesh I would never have bought him a beer. It had to be the Holy Spirit.

He subsequently moved to Portland, Oregon, for a while and then moved to southern Oregon to attend college and make something of his life. He never thought he would see me again, and I never thought I would see him again. He could have moved anywhere in the world. God had allowed us to randomly meet each other again. I have never seen him since. Sometimes it really is a small world. I was completely shocked and walked on clouds with the Holy Spirit for about a month. Of ourselves, we can do nothing. It is God in us who performs His miracles.

Have you ever kept a prayer journal? For one year, I wrote every single request that I asked of the Father. It was just short notes to myself, alongside the date of the prayer so I would remember. I used to write in that journal in the mornings when I walked the beach in Kailua. How I miss that beach. It was beautiful white sand with the sea as warm as bathwater. It began as a pale blue and slowly became a dark aqua, then a beautiful turquoise and on to a deep purple. That was my place to be safe and commune with our Creator. What a wonderful world our God has made.

That journal had many entries. I was always praying about something. At the end of the year, I re-read it and praised God that he did not give me all the requests I thought I needed. Many of my prayers would have brought about drastic results for other people, and even for myself. I couldn't see the entire picture as God did. Many of those prayers would have altered my life in ways that would have prevented me from doing God's will. It would have been my will and my way.

Many times I think I know what I want and what I need, when what I really need is to be silent before the Lord and wait on Him to instill His will in my heart. It always makes me so much happier and ends up being just what my spirit wanted. In my still-childlike approach, I'm looking at things from here without considering what it must look like from God's viewpoint.

It's difficult at times when prayers aren't answered the way I think I need them. Sometimes God permits me to work through whatever problem I have (or someone I'm praying for has). But it gives me the chance to grow from it into a better person.

My very dearest friend—sister by the blood of the Lamb and confidante—is Georgia. We have the same Father. His name is God. She lived on one end of the United States and I live on the other. It was my move, not hers, and it still breaks my heart because I miss the sodas and coffees we had at one another's kitchen tables.

I also really miss her hugs. She was a great hugger. We would sit for hours, speaking of things of the Lord.

I bring this up because her nickname is Raggedy I, and I am Raggedy II. We used those nicknames in emails and when we actually handwrite each other.

She was one of those children of God who never purposefully ministered. It just came naturally to her. She asked me once, "I wonder what it means to pray without ceasing (1 Thessalonians 5:17). How do you do it?"

"You already do it." I told her.

She didn't even know that she was always in a state of prayer. Neither did she know a stranger. Anywhere she went, she started talking to someone about the Lord. And if you didn't want to hear about things of the Lord, you didn't visit her home. She always found a way to get the message of the love of Jesus Christ across to you.

I guess she was one of those people God didn't permit to see how wonderful she really was because her head might have gotten big. Georgia went home to be with our Lord two years ago. I miss her terribly but know she is with the Lord and happy. We will be friends for eternity.

Many years ago, she and I were talking about our sinful natures. We talked about the wonderful gift of Jesus' death on the Cross and the forgiveness that we've never earned or deserved. I brought up the scripture in Isaiah 64:6: *But we are all as an unclean thing, and all our righteousness are as filthy rags; and we all do fade as a leaf; and our iniquities, like the wind, have taken us away.* We discussed that scripture for quite a while and aptly named each other, Raggedy I and Raggedy II. We were filthy rags.

She once asked a few others to join our Raggedy club and told them Raggedy dolls are sometimes hung by one hand, body swinging. . .with heels clunking! Legs flying every which way…being dragged around by the circumstances of life. . .but in the Messiah, we persevere! A little rest, a little sit down, prayer, and we are ready again.

Scripture says the best we can do is still so much less than God does, that our best is still like rags. Raggedys can comment on thoughts of life, or God, or a humorous happening that won't come again, or news of the world that has you thinking or just able to read what is inside another Raggedy.

For Christmas 2004, she mailed me a 36-inch Raggedy Ann and Raggedy Andy doll. I kept them in their boxes for about six months. I was so concerned that this beautiful gift from my loving friend would become damaged or dusty.

Eventually she mailed me a plastic cover for them so I could finally take them out of their boxes and enjoy them.

Several weeks later when she and I talked, she asked if the cover fit the two of them. I didn't have the heart to tell her the truth. In my "Raggedy the lesser" manner I simply told her, "Yes, it fits perfectly." They really did fit, but they were still in their boxes.

I was still afraid that if I took them out, something would happen to them. What if a visiting child wanted to play with them? What if an adult visitor wanted to check them out and soiled them with hands that weren't clean?

Oh, my! I can sure find excuses.

The truth is that they are so precious to me, not because of them, but because of my dear friend whom I love with all my heart and her wonderful kindness in gifting me with them. I had to keep them sealed.

Finally, I had to ask myself if I thought that *if the dolls were ruined or destroyed, our friendship would end.* Of course not! My friend loved me regardless. I have recently taken them out of the boxes to display without the coverings.

Does this remind you of anything? God has given us the absolute best gift anyone will ever give us. He gave us forgiveness, healing, and salvation through His Son, Jesus Christ. What do we do with that gift?

If you're like me, you keep that forgiveness, healing, and salvation wrapped up and you're afraid to use it. I know that I am forgiven and healed by the horrible persecution and death of Jesus Christ. Then I wrap the gift He willingly gave me right back up and put it away so that

I can't even see or feel that wonderful forgiveness and healing myself.

I hide it from my eyes and from everyone else's. I can't even enjoy the liberation and freedom and joy of the gift He gave me.

I wonder how that makes God feel. We must bring grief to His heart. We discount the gift of the pain, suffering, and death of Jesus Christ.

I needed to take those beautiful dolls out of their boxes and display them for everyone to see and enjoy. They needed to become what they were intended to be, a witness to everyone. By displaying them, I'm showing everyone the love and closeness that my Raggedy friend and I shared.

By displaying our wholeness, joy, and forgiveness for others, we are showing the world the forgiveness, healing, and salvation we have because of Jesus Christ. We are also showing the world the wonderful friendship and closeness that the Lord and we share.

It's not simply telling people of His love; *they need to see it!* Sadly, I, like the majority of us, want to see the proof in the pudding. I want to see His love expressed in the lives of other people. Too often we see self-proclaimed Christians walking about with nasty faces and dispositions.

We may work for bosses who manipulate in every way possible to get the best for themselves, never considering they might not even be in their positions without the hard work and efforts of their employees and customers. Have you ever had a boss who is in a different mood every day? Those are the scary ones because you never know what to expect.

There are also employees who are out to take the company for anything they can. They cheat on timecards or waste countless hours doing nonsense instead of productive work.

We might have a neighbor who gossips about everyone while sharing the salvation message. Then, we have those husbands and wives who can't wait for the first opportunity to berate their spouses to another.

We see Christians ridiculing, stealing, lying, and cheating.

We hear about Christian parents abusing their children and even ministers of the Gospel abusing youth.

Now, where is the joy in that?

What kind of salvation is that?

Who would want it? Even we—myself included—who are sinners would reject that kind of religion. I wouldn't want it. Would you? It's a terrible witness of the most wonderful message the world has ever and will ever know.

I guess I was on a bit of a tirade for a few moments. My sin makes me angry. I see myself in so many of those situations, and I hate it.

Paul said in Romans that he hated the sin that he does. *For that which I do I allow not: for what I would that do I not; but what I hate that do I. If then I do that which I would not, I consent unto the law that it is good. Now then it is no more I that do it, but sin that dwelleth in me* (Romans 7:15-17). What Paul was telling us was that he was trying with all his might to live a life according to the Lord, but that he would falter and stumble regardless of his intent.

I completely understand what Paul was saying. I am a Christian, saved not by myself but by the blood, death, and resurrection of Jesus Christ. I should be filled with joy every moment of my life. I should strive to do nothing but the will of God, but sin creeps in and bursts out. After all that is said I must say that, praise God, we have forgiveness. But, we must also hold ourselves accountable for our actions. Forgiveness does not mean that we can go out again and continue to sin. It does not give us free license to continue in our old sinful nature. It simply means that without anything we have done, our gift from God is forgiveness for our sins. What a wonderful gift!

Summary and Reflection
Read Psalms 3 and Proverbs 3

All of us are ragged in some way. We will never fully live up to the Godly potential inside of us all. However, God knows that and chooses to work through us anyway. We need to unwrap that gift and put it on display. It will get dirty and tattered, and sometimes we will really mess up, but our loving God is prepared for that too.

1. What is your passion for witnessing for Christ?
2. Consider that your best deeds are as filthy rags but your worst mistakes are pure white through the blood of Jesus. It is a difficult teaching, but one that can liberate. Consider how you can work to surrender all you do to Christ's multiplication.
3. Pray and ask God who He's placed in your path and how you can minister to them.

Chapter 4
Guilt

Guilt is a self-serving emotion. It does no good thing other than to serve as an excuse for holding onto old failings or indulgences and limiting us. It lowers our self-esteem, and low self-esteem is nothing more than a by-product of guilt. Because of the results of our past and present, we often need a good excuse to have a pity party and not fully participate in the full, blessed life our Father has planned for us. It's much easier to say, "I'm not smart enough; I can't do it right anyway; I don't have time because of 'everything else' I 'have' to do; I've been through too much in my life." It's just a technique that gets us off the hook for commitment to something outside and greater than ourselves.

Guilt immobilizes us. We cannot function well when we are burdened with guilt. It reminds me of a story I was told in my Bible studying years ago. I believe it was about the ancient Romans, but I am not positive. Many years ago, if someone murdered another person, that person's body would be strapped onto the murderer's back and they would have to carry it. There was no taking it off. Eventually, as the dead body decomposed, it would infect the healthy living body and that person would eventually die as a result of the infections. It is the same with guilt and unforgiveness. They will eventually contaminate our healthy body that God has created for His ultimate purpose.

That same guilt and unforgiveness will kill us spiritually and physically. It will contaminate us. Many medical afflictions are the result of negative thinking and guilt. How many people are taking antidepressants, prescribed by a physician? I personally don't believe that's natural. There are times when medically, people need medication but I don't believe it should be a lifetime experience. We punish ourselves by holding onto those self-destructive feelings. God tells us that when we confess (with a sincere heart), our sins are forgiven and never to be remembered. *As far as the east is from the west, so far hath He removed our transgression from us* (Psalm 103:12). There is no meeting of the east and the west. But we continually go back to God and plead for forgiveness for a sin we may have confessed a hundred or a thousand times. I have done that countless times with a sin I committed 45 years ago. I couldn't get rid of the guilt. I finally opened the hearing of my heart to hear God's voice loud and clear. He forgave me 45 years ago, but I never forgave myself. God looks at us, in His infinite love, and asks "What do you mean? I forgave that a long time ago and it is NOT to be remembered."

There is an adage that I find a racist remark, but nonetheless, it is calling someone an "Indian giver." I'm not sure where it originated because the Native Americans are the most giving people I know without any thought for recompense. I am half Native American and very proud of my heritage. My Native American ancestry has helped to shape who I am and even helped to bring me to a closer walk with the Lord. I wonder which half of me is Native American and which half is Lebanese? Can I divide? No, I am uniquely me. But we, as God's children, go to Him and lay our sins at the altar. We give them to Him to be covered by the blood of Jesus and removed. We certainly don't want them. We "gift" God with them. Then we get to thinking about them, pondering them, contemplating His forgiveness. Did he really forgive me of that sin? And here we go, right back to the altar to take them back and wallow in them.

After a bit of time has gone by, we realize again that we need forgiveness, and what do we do? We are right back, laying our sins at the altar and begging forgiveness. We continue to give our precious Lord our sins and take them back and again, returning again and again. We never really give them to Him. We just know what we're supposed to do, so we act it out without the belief in our spirit that He will do as He says.

He will forgive our sins! Scripture says, *God is not a man, that He should lie* (Numbers 23:19a). I believe that all too frequently, as Christians, we look at God as we look at our fellow humans and ourselves. If we were created in His image, then He must be just like us. No! We were created in His image. He was not created in our image. His image was perfection that we have tried to manipulate. We are not exact duplicates. God is not a narcissist, caring only for those who are exactly as He is.

Consider how we act as parents. Our children resemble us in some way and it makes us proud. It is the same with God. We resemble Him and He is proud of us. He never created robots or clones. He never needed to create us for fellowship if He only wanted someone exactly as Himself. But, He wanted us. He desired us. *I will praise thee, for I am fearfully and wonderfully made* (Psalms 139:14a).

He wants companionship and fellowship with each of us. When we begin to have a personal relationship with Christ (and by personal I mean knowing Christ better than you know your own children, spouse, or anyone) you go to Him daily, hourly, sometimes every minute. You get to know Him and crave Him.

Remember back in high school, that first crush, someone you thought you really loved? I remember a crush that I had on a young man when I was a freshman in high school. I thought he was the most handsome and wonderful person I had ever met. His nickname was "Smokey" and I never questioned how he came by that name. Later, when I really got to know him, I learned it was because he was always smoking marijuana. How dumb I was! But there was a time I craved his attention and he failed me (thankfully). But God never fails or falters on His Word. You never stop craving His will. His is the truest, most genuine relationship you will ever have.

We can lay those old thoughts of self-loathing, unforgiveness, guilt, and blame at the foot of the Cross and believe that Jesus Christ can and will cover them with the gift of His blood and eternally wash us from those sins, never to be remembered again. When the old stinking thinking comes back to haunt us, we can say with assurance, "No more. Those sins have been washed by the blood of the Lamb. They are no more! I will not even give a second to entertaining them. They are gone forever." Stand in faith, even if you don't feel like it.

Summary and Reflection

Read Psalms 4 and Proverbs 4

Guilt is a heavy weight we all carry needlessly. Christ died on the Cross once and for all to take every part of our sin from us. That includes the guilt associated with it. However, we are not as quick to forgive as God is. We hold ourselves, and those around us, under the weight of past sins. Many of us hold those sins throughout our lives, never letting go of them. Holding onto those sins will kill us physically and spiritually.

1. The first step to walking from guilt is to realize that Christ's atoning sacrifice covers every aspect of our sin. Do you have any unconfessed sins? Give them to God now and allow Him to wash you clean.

2. Are you living under the rotting carcass of previous wrongs? Consider David. He committed a horrible sin with Bathsheba that had consequences, but God still brought the Messiah from the lineage of David. What can God do through you when you stop weighing your dreams in the shackles of your own guilt?

3. Is there someone else who wants to force you to take back the guilt that you've been liberated from through Christ? Pray for God's leading in how to deal with that relationship or situation and obey. Jesus told us to pray for our enemies so while you wait for Him to answer, spend time daily praying for that person.

Chapter 5
Feelings

You cannot count on feelings because they can be so deceptive. Did you ever feel like you wouldn't like someone at first, only to find the person has since become one of your best friends? Feelings are fickle. You can't depend on them. Don't waver and don't entertain doubts. It doesn't make any difference if you believe it. God said it, and it is so! *That we henceforth be no more children, tossed to and fro...*(Ephesians 4:14a).

If any of you lack wisdom, let him ask of God, that giveth to all men liberally and upbraideth not; and it shall be given him. But let him ask in faith nothing wavering, For he that wavereth is like a wave of the sea driven with the wind and tossed. For let not that man think that he shall receive any thing of the Lord (James 1:5-7).

I remember until recently I suffered guilt from my feelings. I still fall into it at times, but now I rebuke it and claim the Blood of the Lamb. Sometimes I have to keep fighting it over and over. I find myself apologizing for a lot of things that were not my doing. I believe "I'm sorry" is just part of me. If someone was having a bad day, I would wonder what I did to cause it. If my husband was grumpy, I would wonder what I did. If someone didn't like me I always knew it was because I wasn't good enough.

Today I often say "I'm sorry," to end whatever is going on. I do not believe that my ego is large enough that I have to win every disagreement or counter every negative comment that comes my way. If it means ending a problem, I will gladly apologize and permit the person to go on feeling they were correct in their assumption or that they have won. In the larger scheme of things, will it matter who was right and who was wrong on minor things?

I will not, however, compromise my Christian beliefs, morals, or values. Those beliefs I must defend. I am definitely a "black and white" person with little gray. If God says it, then it is so and has to be believed. But if another looks at us and believes that we must push our point on unimportant matters or that we must always be right, what type of witness have we become? That is not a true Christian witness. Neither can we cloud our journey here on earth with stumbling blocks that will trip us or others.

An old saying goes like this: If people say you're a duck and you say "Oh no. I'm not a duck" and they say "Yes you are, you even quack like a duck," well, look to see if you're trailing feathers because you might be a duck. We all need a Christian critic in our lives, and if you don't have one, you better find one. This is not someone who belittles you but someone who will keep you on track with the Lord. I have several in my life and there are times I do not want them speaking to me. I don't want them around, and I try to avoid them. I want to whine and cry and show my anger and self-pity.

They are the ones who gently tell me when I'm off track or beginning to sin or losing sight of my mission. My husband and children are good critics. They gently persuade me. Sometimes, it's not always real gentle. When I fuss and defend myself, they just answer with the Word of God. Ouch! That always hurts. It also serves to wake me up to what I'm doing. Then I have friends whom I have had for many years who will call me and let me know when I'm off the path. Sometimes we'll be in a conversation and I may feel justified in my anger towards another, and all of a sudden, one of them will tell me that I'm letting my feelings and my anger get in the way of seeing or hearing God's will.

They are also the ones who seem to know by our conversations when I haven't been in prayer or quiet before the Lord. My temperament and my attitude change when I haven't been close to my Source. They are the ones who pray for me without ceasing. I Thessalonians 5:16-18 says, *Rejoice evermore. Pray without ceasing. In every thing give thanks: for this is the will of God in Christ Jesus concerning you.*

I remember my ex-husband placing all of his 350-plus pounds on my spine with his hands, as I lay sleeping, and pushing himself up. I knew my back had broken and yet I said "I'm sorry." I didn't even know why I said it. I still have so many back problems because of his actions and yet I thought it was me causing it. He was an abuser and a child molester. I didn't know it when I married him. In fact, I found out in the last 20 minutes of our marriage. That's how long it took for him to walk into the house, for me to confront him, for him to confess and for me to throw his sorry self out.

I married him because I was alone with three children and working a full-time and two part-time jobs. I had hired a live-in babysitter and just felt like I couldn't go on anymore. I was worried my children were thinking the babysitter was becoming their mother and I was exhausted. He was kind and polite and said he loved the Lord. He also manipulated me with guilt. Sometimes when you've become a result of negative actions from others all of your life, evil people can sense it and you become a sort of magnet for the weirdoes of the world. That's what happened to me with him.

I had stopped drinking and drugging and was desperately seeking the Lord. He knew just the right things to say and do. Perhaps if I hadn't had my thinking clouded by the abuse I suffered, I would have become suspicious immediately. However, there is a price to pay for sin. My sin was that I never loved him and I knew it. At our small wedding, everyone said to me, "Why aren't you smiling?" I couldn't smile. I didn't love him. I was not aware that God was trying desperately to stop me. God would have taken care of me and the children if I would have trusted Him. He knew this man was evil and did not come from Him.

All I was hearing was that this man wanted to be in ministry and would help take care of my children and me. He said we would minister together. I just knew there was something wrong with me that I could not love this man who wanted to serve the Lord. The real problem was that we wanted to serve two different Lords. I wanted to serve the God of the universe, the Creator of all things, and he wanted to serve himself. He wanted respectability to pursue his evil desires without anyone knowing. If I had not had an abundance of guilt in my life from accepting all of the guilt that was placed on me, I would have run in the other direction as fast as my short legs would have carried me.

I was sexually abused as a child by my brother and an uncle. I thought I would know all of the warning signs, but I didn't. The ones who abused me were outwardly nasty. *For such are false apostles, deceitful workers, transforming themselves into the apostles of Christ. And no marvel; for satan himself is transformed into an angel of light* (2 Corinthians 11:13-14). I can remember the shame I felt as a little girl when my brother would abuse me. I was abused sexually by him and often while I was asleep. I would wake up and there he was abusing me. I didn't know it was called abuse at that time. I just knew I hated it and believed this was just more punishment that I deserved. I didn't even know at that time in my life (I was only between four and twelve years old) what sex was. If someone would have asked me if I was being sexually abused, I would have said no.

I really don't think that when I was a child, during the late 1940s and 1950s, anyone said the word "sex" out loud, much less explained it to children. I always thought I was so filthy and ugly that I rightfully deserved whatever happened to me. I was afraid to ever tell anyone because I believed I would be beaten, or even worse, given away to a stranger. No matter how bad a situation is, the familiar is always what you're comfortable with.

The few times in my life when I have spoken of the abuse I suffered as a child, people have asked me, "How can you tell us your parents were good people when they permitted this to happen to you?" I honestly do not believe that my parents were aware of anything that happened to me. My father and mother were Godly people and they loved their children. My father would have defended me against anything, if he had known. The problem was that I didn't know my father didn't know. I assumed it was a natural thing, especially for nasty, ugly little girls.

When I began vomiting, my parents took me to many doctors to find out what was wrong. They were concerned and wanted their daughter well. No one ever asked at that time and I never volunteered to tell anyone about my brother. I probably would have gone to my grave keeping all of it secret if the Lord had not come into my life and healed me. My father worked hard all of his life. In the beginning, before my mother became ill with agoraphobia, he was a pilot and my mother was a linguist. After my mother fell ill, my father would accept a position only if they agreed to hire my mother in a position close to him. He always kept her where he could see if she needed him. They loved each deeply and they loved my brother and myself. When my parents were home, no one abused me.

At family dinners, when all of the relatives were over, my uncle always placed himself across the table from me and would stare at me throughout the entire meal. His eyes seemed to hold an evil that I only knew as a child. His eyes told me that I might enjoy myself momentarily at the dinner table, but I would pay a price later. He would abuse me physically, emotionally, and mentally when no one was around. I would become so nervous that I would vomit at the table. I couldn't help it and I couldn't stop it. I never finished a family meal in peace. Sometimes I wondered if my parents thought I was mentally ill or possessed. In my ignorance, I also wondered if there was something mentally wrong with me.

The writing of this chapter has been difficult but in it I have found a total freedom. I am a survivor, but so much more, through the grace and love of my Savior, Jesus Christ. I am complete and fulfilled. No matter what happened, I am no longer scared. The negative memories from my childhood have left. I am left with only the good memories. As the butterfly spreads its wings, after being released from the cocoon, my Lord has brought me forth healed. I have spread my wings in so many ways. Only a total release of myself to Him could have brought this healing. I no longer have to wallow in my own self-pity over experiences from the past. I am a child of God! I am a King's child!

Summary and Reflection

Read Psalms 5 and Proverbs 5

Feelings are fickle things. If we allow them to dictate our life, then our pursuit of God's life for us will be even more difficult. We need to move beyond feelings and focus on faith and trust. Those words will help us as we grow in our walk with Christ.

1.   Set your feelings aside for a moment and read John 3:16-17. Envision your life as if every word of that verse were true. A life with no condemnation and no guilt. Remember that place when feelings of guilt, unworthiness or other negative emotions come back on you.
2.   What feelings are you allowing to rule your life? See what scripture says about them and make a DECISION to believe the scripture and not your feelings.
3.   Get a concordance and look up faith and trust in the Bible. Find no less than 10 scriptures that use each word. Meditate on that throughout the day. This is truth, not feelings.

Chapter 6
Forgiving the Church

On the subject of guilt, along with forgiveness, I want to address forgiving churches. Yes, there are many us who have to forgive different churches. We have gone to church seeking the exact fit where God wants us, only to be met with others filling us with guilt. Don't you wish that God would speak to you in a booming voice that would be unmistakable and just direct you where He wants you? I have tried many churches and denominations, all claiming to be the only true church of God. When I stopped my addictions, the first thought I had was that I needed to be close to the Lord in a church and raising my children in church.

I telephoned several of the churches, not knowing what to ask, other than did they believe Jesus Christ was the living Son of God, born of a virgin; that He came to earth, suffered and died for our sins; and was resurrected on the third day and reigns in Heaven. Of course, they all told me "Yes." Each assured me they were Biblically sound, even the ones that weren't. Oh my! Here I was a brand new Christian and I believed them.

Some of them politely let me know they felt I should attend a different church. Perhaps I was too open when I told them I was a new recovering addict and alcoholic. None of them said outright they didn't want me; they just referred me to a different church. Maybe I was wrong in the belief that they didn't want to deal with anyone in recovery.

It was 1970, and they were still going through some of the 1960s free love and drug generation. Perhaps they thought I would somehow contaminate the body. I don't know if they went through terrible things during the 1960s, so I can no longer hold them at fault. Perhaps they just didn't know what to do. Maybe God was the One leading me elsewhere.

After the period of the 1960s, with free love and drugs everywhere, many thought they could gain wealth and status by becoming ministers. The 1960s generation was a rather lost group of people looking for the right thing to believe in. They were easily misled by all of the seemingly earnest and Godly ministers. However, those ministers were looking for the salvation of their bank accounts and respectability. They weren't looking for the salvation of souls.

I tried every denomination there was, and one by one I came to the belief that it wasn't where I belonged. Some of the churches would have their members gather around me, without warning, and begin rebuking demons out of me. I didn't know what I was supposed to do. Some told me that when the demons came out I would vomit. Well, I couldn't vomit. Believe me, I tried. Boy, did I try! I stopped short of sticking my finger down my throat because then they would know I was faking it and was still demon-possessed.

I would get on my knees daily and beg God to remove these demons from me. Nothing happened! I was feeling more lost than I had ever felt when I was out in the world and actively addicted. And I was beginning to believe old lies that had been told to me. There was no hope for me. Even God wouldn't deliver me from this ugly, nasty, demon-filled person I had become and probably always would be.

One church, a very large and well-known denomination, brought a lot of suspicions to my mind. The members seemed wonderful, almost angelic in their actions and demeanor. They sent two young missionary men over to minister to me. They even mowed my lawn every week.

I was just beside myself thinking how wonderful they were and how I was being blessed. Then they told me it was time for me to join the church and that I needed to speak with their bishop. I was ready because I had a few questions. They said they believed Jesus was the true Son of God b-u-t there was also this other man they were claiming was the true son of God. Did I misunderstand?

The night before my scheduled visit with their bishop, I got on my knees and prayed and prayed and prayed. I opened the Bible and just placed my hand on the page with a scripture I had seen: *Prove all things; hold fast that which is good* (1 Thessalonians 5:21). In my praying I said, "Lord, I don't understand what I'm supposed to do and where I'm supposed to be. I just know I want to go to Your church and serve You instead of the devil. These people who were here seem so nice, but You said to test all things. I don't know how to do that so I'm going to ask You to do that and show me clearly because I'm so dumb I might not understand."

When I went to the church that evening, I really saw what God was telling me in no uncertain terms. Loud and clear! My three children and my mother had gone along with me and my mother said she would wait in the car with the children while I was in my appointment. I went in to meet the bishop and was a nervous wreck thinking they might not want me when they found out how bad I was. The bishop was gracious and seemed kind and gentle— again, almost angelic. I asked some questions about Jesus and he seemed to answer everything correctly. Then he told me it was God's will that I marry one of the men in the church and continue having children. (My, oh my!) God hadn't told me about that and I was really getting nervous.

One thing I know is that God is a gentleman. He will never reveal to another what He hasn't revealed to you. Everything went downhill from there. Suddenly there was a knock on his office door. I didn't notice anyone else in the church when I came in and wondered who it might be. He chose to ignore it and kept talking. The knock grew increasingly louder and I heard my mother's voice calling my name. I started to get up to answer it and he said to just sit and relax, someone would take care of it. Then I heard the urgency in her voice and rushed to open the door. Things were getting strange.

As the door opened, my mother said, "They're shooting at each other!" I started to ask what she was talking about when I noticed my children, almost blended into the carpet under the pews, and looking terrified. I asked, "Where are they?" She said, "Outside the door." I ran to the door while the bishop was requesting that I come back into his office and continue the conversation saying it would all be okay. No way was this going to be okay! I bent down to put the bottom lock on the door, so the gunmen wouldn't get in and had my head bent when suddenly the door burst open and I felt the barrel of a gun jammed into my head. I yelled "Lord, I'm coming home and I haven't even been baptized!"

Reflecting on that many years later, I can laugh, but at the time I was terrified that finally in my life I had gotten something right and now I was going to be killed before I was baptized. Actually, it was the police and they thought I was one of the gunmen. The bishop asked all of us, my precious mother, children and me to come into a particular room where we would be safe. We hurried in and he shut the door and locked us in, he said for our safety. Guess who was in the room with us? One of the gunmen, hiding. I almost broke the door down getting us all out. The police somehow arrested him and we were safe. Let me tell you, I have never gone back to that denomination and always try to warn others away from it.

In my childish way, I had asked the Lord for help, and did He ever answer me. We later learned that the men began a gun battle over drugs and one ran into the church, with the other following. I was just glad to be done with it.

I continued my journey seeking the right church once again. There were many churches that we attended and some that we joined. Some were way over the edge and others were fine. One church that we briefly attended brought my eldest daughter to the front of the church, while I was at home one evening and demanded that she confess her sins to the church. She was only fifteen and an innocent child. She confessed the usual sins of a young teen, disobeying parents, staying up late, not doing homework but there was no end to their search for demons. They traumatized her and she never wanted to attend church after that experience.

That pastor also stole my car and later was arrested by the F.B.I. Apparently he was wanted in a number of states for conning people out of their property and money. Many who we think are Christians are only agents of the devil and his self-serving followers. Try the spirits, ask God to test them! Don't follow blindly.

We did eventually find good, sound churches that preached an uncompromised Word of God. God was always there taking care of us through the bad churches and the good churches. He taught me what a true Christian was. I learned more from fellowshipping with God and my Bible than I did from any man, woman, or church.

Today, we are all in a good church that preaches the uncompromised message and calls each of us to follow and be active in the ministry God has ordained for our lives.

Our pastor is a young man with a vision of seeing the world saved for Jesus Christ. He doesn't want pampered babies in the Church continuing on pabulum and only ministering to those already seated in the pews. He wants us all to mature as Christians and serve God and humanity. He encourages our ministries and wants us to grow in the Word and in our faith. He wants us off the milk bottle and into the solid meat of God's Word. He is truly a Shepherd. The members of our church support each other like true brothers and sisters. I have never heard gossip or negative comments.

When I attend church, I feel like I'm coming home. It's welcoming and I get the feeling that I'm wanted there and even needed a little bit. We have several people in the church who bless me each time I see them. One is Mary; she is such a strong woman in the Lord and has never failed to bless me. She will say just the right thing to me at just the right time. Mary does not see herself as a preacher, she thinks God has called her to teach, but I can see her going all over the world one day to preach the unadulterated Word of God.

Another has something about her spiritually that I can only describe as "cuteness." The Lord placed it in her to minister to many people. She is just finishing university and is working towards a divinity degree and has now been hired as a hospital chaplain. Sometimes she opens her mouth to say certain things and it's not her speaking on her own, but the Lord speaking through her. What I find wonderful is that she is not aware of it at all. She is simple, in a beautiful way, kind of like the apostles must have been.

We also have another minister at church who is our prayer warrior. If a church doesn't have a prayer warrior, they better find one quickly. And can she pray! Whenever someone wants someone to pray, I offer a quick prayer that she will be the one of the people praying. She just gets us all praising the Lord! She doesn't think she's very intelligent, but when she opens her mouth, the wisdom of the Lord pours forth.

Summary and Reflection

Read Psalms 6:1-10 and Proverbs 6:1-35

Churches are made up of people. People are imperfect. There are many people who have experienced hurt as a result of people who claimed to be in relationship with Christ but weren't. Jesus is waiting for us to come to Him. He loves us. And I know that even during this time, I was growing in Him. He was building me up and helping me through these difficult times and led me to a body who would truly love me.

1. If you've ever been hurt by someone in the Church or someone you know who was a Christian? Are you blaming God for their actions?
2. Consider a time when you've tried to follow God's will but seemed to be dogged at every step. Look at how you grew as a result.
3. Proverbs is a book of wisdom and Psalms is a book of Praise. Read over the six Psalms and Proverbs we've read this week. What has God taught you through them? Which has been particularly meaningful to you?
4. Consider the people in your church that have blessed you and who you have blessed. Do they outnumber those who might have hurt you? If so, then you are doing well, if not you might not be where the Lord wants you to be. Pray for and forgive those who have hurt you as well as those who have blessed you.

Chapter 7
Other Stressors

I also want to address teachers and professors from our past or present whom we need to forgive. As I have already mentioned, when I was in first grade, I began vomiting on my desk. I really don't know why it happened, it just did. I would wake in the middle of the night and vomit without warning. I believe it resulted from all the abuse I was experiencing from my mother's sister and brother. I can still remember being embarrassed by my first grade teacher because of it. She would also belittle me because I couldn't write. I would try over and over at home to practice but I just couldn't do it. My brother would sit with me and help me and eventually I learned and was proud of myself for being able to do it, and was thankful to him. After that time I always had excellent penmanship. It was important to me because it meant I wasn't so bad after all.

There were many things I had difficulty with in those early years, and I came to be thought of as learning disabled, but that term was not used at the time. The teachers either thought you were just stupid naturally or you weren't trying hard enough.

Neither of those was correct about me. I wasn't stupid and I certainly did work at trying to learn. However, comments from the nuns aided in my concept of myself as being less than everyone else. My brother's high intelligence didn't help me either. I am certainly not faulting him for being intelligent. I was jealous and wished I could learn easier.

Throughout my childhood, my brother had broken my nose walls about twelve times before I was twelve years old. That meant my nose was packed and taped. It seemed like it always was. It would begin hemorrhaging after my brother would beat me in the face. It seemed that nothing stopped it. When this happened, my parents would take me to the hospital, where they would pack and tape my nose.

It seemed that until I reached thirteen or fourteen, I felt like an ugly kid with a taped face. I hated it. I didn't want to go out of the house, or to school, or anywhere. I just knew everyone was staring at me and laughing. In those days no one ever asked children about things that happened at home. I don't know if my parents were ever questioned about it or not or if they were really aware of what was happening. I doubt it. I know I never told them. I probably thought my father would have killed anyone that harmed me.

All of the events made me feel inferior and believe that nothing good would ever happen. I used to wonder why my parents never did anything to stop the beatings from my brother, one aunt, and one uncle. I now know, because of my mother's background and upbringing, they simply couldn't do anything else. It was all they knew. My father's Native American ancestry was matriarchal. The husband left his family and became part of the wife's family and culture. I do not believe that my father ever looked back, other than to visit his family once or twice when my brother and I were children. My aunt used to tell my brother that he was better looking than Jesus Christ. I wonder now how that must have skewed him emotionally as a child and later as an adult. None of us knew or understood mental illness in the 1940s and 1950s.

I never understood why my brother was so angry and so abusive. When he turned 18 or 19 years old, he was diagnosed with schizophrenia, which quickly escalated. As he aged, he became increasingly violent, with most of his anger aimed at me. Later, after I was married and had children, he would come to my home and stand in the street and scream that I was the bride of satan. Because I was related to him and because he would hurl abuses at me, I thought something was wrong with me. I knew inside that everyone else thought it too.

My mother suffered from terrible guilt because of her son and attempted to compensate by telling me that I should try to understand him and be kind to him. Once, as an adult, I had saved enough money for a new sofa and brought it home, my brother stood in the street screaming that I was the devil because I always had everything. My mother begged me to give my brother the sofa, saying she would purchase another one for me. I didn't realize, at the time, the guilt and fear my mother suffered because of my brother's schizophrenia. She always believed that somehow she caused the schizophrenia. At that time, many believed schizophrenia was inherited thru the mother.

My brother had beautiful things that my mother bought for him and his family but they never respected those things. My father always said, "Whatever you get free, you'll never appreciate." He was right in those words; my brother, his wife, and children never took care of anything. They destroyed everything they ever had. But, I still was not healed and felt that I deserved nothing, so I became the dutiful child trying to win approval from my mother and my brother while feeling anger deep inside that never went away and only added more guilt.

When I was in college, I had a professor whom I could not seem to learn from. He was really a nice person but looked like and acted like a famous comedian. Everyone loved him because he was so funny (even I did). However, he taught Statistics and when he brought the comedy into the classroom, I had difficulty learning the subject matter. He would give us various problems and then write the answer on the board or work the problem to its conclusion.

At that same time, I was also taking a learning and memory course from him. We were learning how we learn, what the brain actually does to bring about the learning process, and the process of memory. It was a difficult class. I was a serious student and did not have time for humor while learning. I have always loved to laugh but not during classes. Maintaining a high grade-point average was too important to me. I think I needed to prove myself to myself.

During this particular professor's class, I also had a reaction to a medication my physician had given me. I lost part of my memory for a few days. It happened the day of exams. I knew the subject matter perfectly. I had studied long and hard for the exam but when I looked at the exam sheet, I knew nothing. Not one thing came to my mind, not even the name of the professor. I tried and tried to recall his name to place on the exam and couldn't do it. I finally went to him and asked if I could take the exam in a quiet room. He said yes and escorted me to another room. I thought the quiet would help, but it didn't. I finally had to turn the test in without one correct answer.

I wasn't sure what was happening to me but when I couldn't even figure out how to get home after the class, I knew I was in trouble. Fortunately my cell phone had my doctor's number in it and my home number. My husband came and picked me up and took me to the doctor. The doctor told me what I was suffering was a side effect of the medication. She warned me to never take it again. I didn't fail his class but I certainly did not get the grade I wanted, even though it was a B. I was disappointed in myself. I was still judging myself according to what I thought was the world's standards.

Toward the end of the term, I was discussing this with the professor. I told him that I wanted to go to graduate school and would like to begin applying. He said not to bother, explaining how difficult grad school was and that I would have a great deal of difficulty even if I was accepted. I was devastated and considered quitting right then and not graduating or even bothering to apply. Here I was, on several honor societies and felt I had only made it by the skin of my teeth through his class.

When we moved to Oklahoma, my desire to go to graduate school was even stronger. My husband encouraged me to go. He told me I had nothing to lose. If I failed, it wouldn't change anything and nobody would need to know. Bless him; he believed I would succeed. We all need someone who believes in us. I applied to the University of Oklahoma and was accepted. I completed the master's program in about one and a half years with almost a 4.0 average.

I was thrilled and had to email my old professor to tell him. I also told him how I almost didn't try because of his comments. He replied immediately and said he was shocked that he had said that. He said he always thought I was an excellent student who worked very hard, and he must have been having a bad day. I was still ready to accept negative that was said about me. In spite of the hard work I did with my studies I still believed it was mostly luck and certainly not my doing. I still didn't believe I was intelligent enough. All of us have insecurities, whether they are real or imagined, that haunt us throughout our lives. The only way we can get rid of the insecurities and stressors is by giving them to God and working our hardest.

God taught me forgiveness for him also. God also taught me in that moment to watch my words to others and to always ask Him to station an angel at the doorway of my mouth (Psalms 141:3). I was sad when I learned the professor's contract was not renewed. I believe he could have been a credit to the university.

We all have experiences that make us want to stop trying or just give up. If we stop, we will stagnate and never reach the potential that the Lord knows we can achieve and wants us to achieve.

Summary and Reflection
Read Psalms 7 and Proverbs 7

Everyone has stressors in their life. For some, it is the unkind words of a loved one. For others, the stress comes from the number of activities they are trying to jam into each day. Whatever they are, we need to remember that Jesus is there, waiting, to relieve us of our stress. The Bible says, "The chastisement of our peace was upon him." That means everything that causes you problems was dealt with on Calvary. Remember that when stress tries to steal your focus.

1. Do you have stressors in your life that are distracting you from God's love? Step back and give them to Him.

2. Everyone has a story. Mine was abuse (from others and myself) but yours might have been something else. No matter what the stressors of your life have been they can be overcome with God's love. Find a scripture that deals with the root of your issue and meditate on God's healing promises to you.

3. Write down at least three times where what looked to be a tragedy turned in to a triumph. Next write down three places where your worst fears didn't actually happen. How much time was wasted in fear during these times when you could have trusted in God during those times? Don't worry. We all fall short and God loves us just the same. Allow Him to remove one stressor from your life now.

Chapter 8
Choosing Healing

Have you chosen healing? What? Some of you are thinking, "Is this person for real? Of course, I choose healing." Not so fast. We do not always "choose" healing. We may be at that point where we truly do choose it, and that is wonderful. But for many of us, healing is not really comfortable, even though we "think" we want it. Often it's difficult to really want to be healed. Being healed carries its own set of responsibilities and life change. We can't expect others to wait on us. We cannot lie around the majority of the day *because* we are too ill or incapacitated to do those things that need to be done. We cannot expect others to feel sympathy for us. We cannot expect to do the same actions continuously and have a different outcome. We can't always trust our thoughts. Remember when Peter "thought" he knew the Lord's will, in the garden?" He sliced off the high priest's servant's ear (Matthew 26:51). Was that really the Lord's will? Nope! Jesus had to heal the man's ear.

Often we bring extra work to God when we think we know—instead of *really* knowing—God's will. It is the same with healing. We think we want to be healed, but we've become too comfortable in our need. We want to continue our lives as they are, but remove the bad consequences. We can excuse ourselves from many demands. We want the immediate outcome to change. We don't want all the bills that we have charged. We don't want the illness that comes with our unhealthy lifestyles. But, we don't want to take the effort to change. We want to continue putting in what we always have. Have you ever heard, nothing changes if nothing changes?

We feel sorry for ourselves and appeasement is all we want. It's a downward spiral. What do you mean that I have to exercise and eat right and stay away from certain things to be healthy? *I want what I want!* Who does my boss think she/he is to talk to me that way or tell me to do whatever? *I want respect and I want it right now!* Who does my husband/wife think they are to tell me the house needs attention, or that I have to cook or mow the lawn? *I want what I want when I want it!* Who does my pastor or who do the elders think they are to tell me that I should be fellowshipping at church on certain days or that I should tithe? *I'll go where I want and do what I want with my money when I feel like it!*

Have you gotten the idea that we may not want to get out of our comfort zone? What part of me is my responsibility and what part is God's responsibility? The emotional symptoms that we experience today come from a memory source that we have perceived in a certain way which harmed or formed us. We cannot force them out of the way or force them to leave. They are a part of us and they are also part of what has shaped our lives and made us, us, good and bad so far. We can now choose to look at them and open the way for God's healing to come in.

There is a process to this. God can step in immediately and heal our hurts but the consequences of those hurts may take longer to work through. First, know that NOTHING will change our past. Our past is behind us. It is a place we cannot revisit; nor would most of us want to. I wouldn't! Nothing will change the actions of the past. But God can use that past, no matter how horrible, to change our future to be in line with His will. *It is God's will that our souls should prosper and that we know good health* (3 John 2). When that scripture is read, people usually assume that "prosper" means financially. There are many ways to prosper. When I pray for someone, and often for a total stranger, I always ask God to prosper them in every way, first spiritually, then emotionally, then physically, then financially. I believe that spiritual prosperity is the most important. If we have spiritual prosperity, the rest will fall into place. We will seek God's will and His instructions. It is in following those instructions that He can lead us to prosperity in other areas.

At the beginning, we may have anxiety. You cannot stop feeling anxious, but God gives us a way to overcome it. The Bible tells us "Do not be worried or anxious…" but there are times when anxious thoughts creep into our heads. *Be careful for nothing; but in every thing by prayer and supplication with thanksgiving let your requests be made know unto God* (Philippians 4:6). There have been many times when anxiety has crept over me and it feels as though my heart is trembling. I pray and pray, and it doesn't seem to go away. Then, suddenly it's gone and I am able to feel peace again. I believe that is when I become distracted by something else and the Holy Spirit is able to release me from the feelings of anxiety. The anxiety will come from experiences of feeling rejected, or feeling that you will fail, or perhaps just from low self-esteem. These are only memories from our past and really cannot hurt us today. However, they do affect us. Our memories have made us what we are and how we see ourselves. For many people— maybe you—your memories are heavy baggage. Anxiety can also come from fear, and fear never comes from God. Take control of fear and memories by using your faith in Jesus Christ. They are simply old movies replaying in your mind. They are ways you are attempting to protect yourself.

Remember Psalm 23:4, *Yea, tho I walk through the valley of the shadow of death, I will fear no evil [real or imagined], for thou art with me.* Praise God for that scripture! I will fear nothing!!! What a releasing scripture! What a wonderful motto for our lives. *A man's heart deviseth his way: but the Lord directeth his steps* (Proverbs 16:9). *I can do all things through Christ which strengtheneth me* (Philippians 4:13). You can do anything and everything through Christ Jesus!

You can be healed from the hurts of your past because God is with you and He will direct you! Know this and get it into your spirit! Do not be afraid to change anything in your life to line up with the plan God has made for your life. There are no mistakes when we surrender to His will and His word! Do not be afraid that there is anything you cannot do.

Summary and Reflections
Read Psalms 8 and Proverbs 8

It is easy for us to say that we choose healing, but the process of healing can be a bit more difficult. Despite this, healing has been God's plan since He spoke to the Israelites in the wilderness and said: "*I call this day against you, that I have set before you life and death, blessing and cursing: therefore choose life, that both thou and thy seed may live* (Deuteronomy 30:19).

1.   What unhealthy things are you holding on to that are stopping the flow of God's healing touch? It may be attitudes, relationships, activities or other things.

2.   Place these unhealthy things before God's throne and ask Him for deliverance from them. The deliverance may not come immediately, but as you trust God's promise to heal you, things will begin to change. Trust that what God has promised, He will do.

3.   Speak life, health, and healing into those around you. Speak blessing not cursing into your own life as well. The Bible urges us to watch our tongue. Take notes of the negative and damaging [which is the opposite of healing] words that come from your mouth. Repent of those and ask God to put a door on your mouth. Read Proverbs 13.

4.   Make a list of everyone you can remember hurting you or who has reacted to you in any way that would have dug itself into your subconscious. Take your time with this. Perhaps carry a little notebook with you and jot names or situations down as you remember them. Ask God to bring those names to your remembrance. If it was an action and you don't know the person's name, briefly jot down the action. This is only for your eyes and God's eyes.

Don't be ashamed to write anything down. God already knows it all. No one else will ever see it. Let it take as long as it needs.

5. When you're finished with the list, pray about each item on it. Pray and ask God to help you release and forgive the person or the action of another. You don't need to understand why someone hurt you. We are all responsible for our own actions. God has asked us to forgive, He didn't ask us to understand. *Forbearing one another, and forgiving one another, if any man have a quarrel against any: even as Christ forgave you, so also do ye* (Colossians 3:13). The Lord did not ask us to explain our actions when He forgave us; He asked us to confess our sins and ask forgiveness and He would be quick to forgive us.

Chapter 9
Forgiveness

Take out the list that you made in Chapter Eight. Now hold the page(s) you filled in your hands and ask God to forgive all of these people and actions for you and through you. It doesn't make any difference if you feel like forgiving them right now. Just do it because God asked you to forgive them. *Then came Peter to him, and said, Lord, how oft shall my brother sin against me, and I forgive him? Till seven times? Jesus sayeth unto him, I say not unto thee, Until seven times: but, until seventy times seven* (Matthew 18:21-22). That's 490 times. WOW! God forgives those who have no right to be forgiven. He even forgives those who hate Him. He forgives us! You are a King's kid. Act like a King's kid.

> *And forgive us our debts [sins], as we forgive our debtors [those who sin against us]* (Matthew 6:12).
> *But I say unto you, that every idle word that men shall speak, they shall give account thereof in the day of judgment* (Matthew 12:36).
> *For if you forgive men when they sin against you, your heavenly Father will also forgive you. But if you do not forgive men their sins, your Father will not forgive your sins* (Matthew 6:14-15).
> *Forbearing one another, and forgiving one another, if any man have a quarrel against any: even as Christ forgave you, so also do ye* (Colossians 3:13).
> *But I say unto you, love your enemies, bless them that curse you, do could to them that hate you, and pray for them which despitefully use you, and persecute you that ye*

may be the children of your Father, which is in heaven
(Matthew 5:44-45a).

*He that sayeth that he is in the light, and hateth his
brother, is in darkness even until now. He that loveth his
brother abideth in the light, and there is none occasion of
stumbling in him. But he that hateth his brother is in
darkness, and walketh in darkness, and knoweth not
whither he goeth, because that darkness hath blinded his
eyes* (1 John 2:9-11).

Courageously give your life a long look. Where has
unforgiveness or hatred brought you? Being wronged by
another is no justification for unforgiveness. If this were so,
Jesus would have every reason to hate each of us instead of
loving us with His unrelenting love.

He gave His life for us.

Did the soldiers kill Jesus? No, each of us did with
our sins and our unforgiveness for each other.

Have any of us been perfect? There is no one
perfect but Jesus Christ.

Several years ago, I had a traumatic experience in
my life that involved a person and a pastor who just wasn't
very experienced. It hurt my heart so deeply that I never
wanted to return to church. I wasn't angry with God, but I
was terribly angry and hurt with the person who performed
the action and with the advice the pastor had given me.

I was filled with such hurt and such unforgiveness
for myself and for those who had been hurt by this person
that I could not pray for almost three months. Finally, I
began to pray because I knew how lonely my heart was for
my Father and my Lord.

Despite my anger, I knew God was the only one
who could perform a healing within me. I hated the feelings
I was experiencing. I began to pray, and it was as though
the heavens had turned to brass. My prayers felt like they

were bouncing back at me and going nowhere. I remember crying out, "Were You ever there? Were You a lie all along? Was it just me thinking there was a God?"

My being was hurt to its very core. My soul hurt! I had always prayed and it always brought me great peace and joy, but now, all it brought was deep pain. However, I kept praying because I knew that was what I should be doing. I did retain that much of my senses.

After a few months of no response, I thought "Why pray any longer. It's no use." Suddenly I heard in my heart, "Act as if." I thought "What?" I wondered where this thought was coming from. And again I heard, "Act as if." Eventually God's words sank through my unforgiving heart and I began to pray "as if" I felt Him and His presence.

I was faking it because I felt nothing. After a short while, I was on my knees one evening and poured my heart out to God in earnest. The tears flowed until I trembled with emotion. Suddenly, I felt my prayers break through to the Heavenly throne. What a relief! What joy I felt! It was then that I could begin to forgive. That didn't mean I *had* forgiven, but I gave God power to change my will in this matter and it was the beginning of healing.

Was God there when I felt the heavens had turned to brass? Of course, He was. It wasn't God who had moved. It was me who had moved from His presence and away from His umbrella of protection. By my hurt and unforgiveness, I had willingly taken myself away from God. I was feeling hatred toward a person, and that hatred would have killed me. It had already begun to poison me spiritually. That spiritual decay also began to become a physical decline within me. If I had held onto that anger and hatred and not given God permission to change my will, I believe that I would have perished physically.

If you do not feel like forgiving those in your life who have or are hurting you, *act as if.* Just do what the Creator told us to do. He is the one with the blueprint of life. We hold no patents on Creation. When all else fails, follow the Master's directions. Give God the permission to change your will. Remember that God has given each of us free will, and He will not go against it.

My eldest daughter recently made me laugh when she said, "This free will is not all it's cracked up to be. It can sure get you into trouble." But because of that same free will, we have the right to ask God to change our will. Our will has given Him permission. Can you try it now? Hold the paper with so many names on it in your hands and ask God to forgive them for you. Our precious Lord never asks us to do the impossible. All He asks is for us to have a willingness to let Him make us willing to forgive others.

Summary and Reflections

And ye shall know the truth, and the truth shall make you free (John 8:32).

And I will pray the Father and he shall give you another Comforter, that he may abide with you for ever: Even the Spirit of truth; whom the world cannot receive because it seeth him not, neither knoweth him; but ye know him; for he dwelleth with you, and shall be in you (John 14:16-17).

Howbeit when he, the Spirit of truth, is come, he will guide you into all truth: for he shall not speak of himself; but whatsoever he shall hear, that shall he speak: and he will shew you things to come. He shall glorify me: for he shall receive of mine, and shall shew it unto you. All things that the Father hath are mine: therefore said I, that he shall take of mine, and shall shew it unto you (John 16:13-15).

Total surrender comes first and foremost to the Christian. The more truth we know, the freer we become.

Submit means to come under order or command, to come in harmony with. It means "submission when it doesn't even make sense."

Resist means to stand against something in an active manner.

When you cannot forgive, "act as if." Permit God to handle the rest. Satan does not want us to seek forgiveness or to freely give it. He has the power of death, and that is what he wants you to receive. God has the power of life, and that is what He wants you to receive freely from Him. Decide which you want.

In your notes, write that you choose life, you choose salvation, and you choose Jesus Christ as your Lord and Savior! Keep that note and look at it frequently. This is a freewill choice.

Chapter 10
Hearing God's Voice

I had an aunt as a child who was particularly abusive to me. She never cared for females and I could never understand the logic of that thinking since she was a woman. She took care of my brother and I while our parents worked.

There were many times I suffered as a result of her actions and her words. I have never known what transpired in her own life as a child to cause those feelings. Somehow, today, I believe she was raised as I was, with abuse from someone.

One of the many things she used to do while I was napping was to sneak into my room, tiptoe to the bed, and ever so quietly get hold of the top layer of the skin on my back and pinch me while digging her long nails in until I bled. Just a tiny amount of skin, but it caused much physical and emotional pain in my young body and mind.

I always heard her come in because I faked my naps. I was actually afraid to go to sleep. Somehow, in my childish thinking, I thought if I ever really did fall asleep, she would kill me.

I had grown into adulthood, physically, not spiritually, and had children of my own when my aunt suffered a terrible stroke. She could no longer speak properly; it was called aphasia. She would try her hardest to say something but something totally unrelated—and often, not nice—would come out instead. It frustrated her horribly. She had already given all of her considerable wealth to my brother and one male cousin and now had little or nothing left.

No one in the family wanted to take care of her. They all begged out for various reasons. Life was too busy for them; they had children at home; they didn't have enough money to bring someone else in, or just not enough energy.

I don't know if it was the Lord telling me to bring her to live with me or not, but I felt that I should. Of course, I always wanted her to like me. Perhaps I thought this might finally bring approval and love from her.

I flew to California, where she was still in the hospital, and made arrangements to bring her back to Oregon with me. I had three children, and my mother living in our three-bedroom home. I bought a bed for her and put her in my mother's room and went about taking care of her, content in the hope of her loving me.

I cooked her meals and carefully washed and ironed her clothing. One day after I had finished bathing her in the shower, I knelt down to rub lotion on her feet. I was massaging them when suddenly I felt something I hadn't felt since I was a child. She dug those beautiful, but horrible, long nails into my back and drew blood.

I was shocked. All of my horrible childhood memories flooded back into my mind. I could not believe that no matter what I did for her, thinking it was out of love, she still hated me. I quickly finished putting on her lotion, got her dressed, and made her comfortable in the family room with my mother.

My mother noticed I was upset and asked if I was all right. I said that I was fine but needed to do some things in my room. I went directly to my bedroom, locked the door and got on my knees. By this time, I believed I was a good Christian woman. I had forgiven all.

On my knees, I cried to the Lord for about four hours. I cried and I sobbed. I shed so many tears that I thought Noah must have been outside rebuilding the ark. I shook and trembled and called out:

"Why? Why have You permitted this? I tried to love her. I've tried to minister to her. I've done everything I could for her."

I, I, I. That's all God was hearing. After about four hours, God must have gotten tired of hearing this whiny baby girl complaining. It was then that I heard His voice as though it were booming and audible. He said, "You are not ministering to her! She is ministering to you!"

It was as though someone had slapped me and awakened me from a long, deep sleep. Indeed, she had been ministering to me my entire life. Did I like it? Absolutely not! Was I relieved and thrilled to hear all of the abuse was her way of ministering to special me? No way! Did I check this out and make sure it was God's voice I heard and not the devil's? You better believe it! I prayed for a long time after that. I needed confirmation on this one!

God will never lead you against His Word. If He says it, you will find confirmation in the Word of God. He is the potter and we are the clay. God has always refined us through the fire, like fine gold, and that's exactly what God showed me. He was refining me so He could use me for His purpose.

In reality, I really hadn't comprehended God's way of forgiving at all. I was patting myself on the back while holding onto all the anger and bitterness. God wasn't finished with me yet. Do you think He ever grows weary with us? Trying to raise us? No, thankfully, He never grows weary!

Does all of this mean that God wanted my aunt to abuse me? No. He never once wanted that to happen.

After I wrote this about my aunt, my youngest daughter called and I read it to her. I was excited because God had revealed to me that indeed I would be thrilled to see my aunt in heaven. What a healing and blessing that was for me!

My daughter asked me "Mom, if someone else were reading this, which they will be, do you want them to think the abuse was okay and that they should be thrilled to see their abusers? Also, because you went through this abuse, does it make you want to do things or concede to things for others just so they'll like you? You wanted her to love you so much and never got that love. Do you do things to cause others to love you now because you need it so badly?"

Wow! That child can sure ask some direct questions at times. I thought about it and said no, I don't feel that way. Neither would I want others to feel they need to be thrilled or even desire to see their abusers again, or to ever be hurt by anyone. Abuse of any kind is a horrible experience. It is an experience that can tear a child's self-esteem from them and cause a lifelong trail of problems. This is just the way God has worked in my life. Yes, I always wanted my aunt to love me, and I would love to see her in heaven, a new creature in Jesus Christ—but if she isn't there, and if that love is never given to me, it won't matter. It simply won't matter any longer. What matters is what God has done in my heart. He has given me the ability to finally forgive. *To whom ye forgive anything, I forgive also* (2 Corinthians 2:10a). I have found that in forgiving others, God can truly forgive me and I can forgive myself.

As for doing things in my life to bring about love from others, yes, I did do that. I would put up with a great deal from people just to get them to like me. It was important that I be liked. I remember having difficulty being frank with people. It terrified me. I was so afraid of rejection that I even encouraged additional abuse in my life.

Some people might wonder why my parents didn't seem to protect me and stop the abuse. They were dependent on my mother's family because of my mother's agoraphobia. My mother was raised in the same environment I was. My mother endured many abuses of her own from her family. My father loved us completely, but he was a product of an abusive and drunken father. I don't think either of them knew how to stop it or even completely recognize it. I also believe my father, in many ways, was afraid of my mother's family.

I would choose men whom I never loved and who were unworthy of me, just to avoid being alone. Often they, too, abused me physically or mentally. That was all I knew and that was what I was comfortable with. I just thought "This is life." I remember a song by Peggy Lee, "Is that all there is?"

I always related to that dismal song, and yet hated it. In it she sang about coming to the conclusion that there isn't much to life and nothing to look forward to at the end of life. I never questioned if other women, or even men, were also abused. I assumed everyone was, especially women, and it was never discussed. Abuse was normal for me. Love—true, unconditional love—was abnormal. That caused a problem when others told me that God's love was true and unconditional. I couldn't understand, it even though I thought I did. Those who I thought were my friends at the time only used me. They probably thought I was wishy-washy and would do anything to keep them, and they were probably right.

I remember always wanting to die. Many times I awoke with the thought, "Today is a good day to die." I couldn't get rid of the thought. I didn't want to go through the painful process of death, and I sure didn't want to leave my children for someone else to love, but I just wanted to die. I never saw life getting any better. All I could relate to was growing to 70 or 80 years old and continuing as a second- or even third-class person. I was not worthy of anything good. I hated myself. I didn't speak well. I wasn't intelligent. I wasn't pretty, and I certainly wasn't shaped well.

People tell me today that I am outspoken and direct. Yes, I am outspoken but never to hurt another. I am always an advocate of those who are oppressed. I know too well what the hurt of someone's mouth can do. I do not ever want to be the cause of another child of God feeling that way because of me.

Today I can count my true close friends on one hand. They are people who are mature in the Lord. They are people who love me unconditionally, not because of me, but because of God in me. They support me and they instruct me, especially when they think I'm doing something God would not have me do. They are also the first to encourage me when I need it and when I'm trying to follow God's will for my life.

They are my confidantes. They are my friends, and I have been blessed to have them in my life. As it has turned out, six of my best friends and best supporters have been my husband Sanford, my three children, Sabrina, Michael (a.k.a. Sanford II), DeAnna, and my two grandsons, Scott and Micah.

Raggedy I—Georgia, my best friend—always encouraged me as well. She would always get a little pushy, but I loved her.

They make me laugh. They are always there for me, but they also are instrumental in instructing me in the ways of the Lord. I have truly been blessed. When I believed I was too dense to finish high school when I was 49 years old, it was my husband and children and even my grandsons, Scott and Micah, who encouraged me to do it. They encouraged (I could say coerced!) me to get my bachelor's degree and my master's degree. When I felt I couldn't go on, they were my cheerleaders. They celebrated every "A" and "B" grade that I received. When I made the honor rolls or was asked to join certain academic honor societies, they would tell me what a good job I was doing. They wanted the best for me.

Isn't that what a true friend is—one who always wants what is best for you, even if it means they're doing without the things you usually do with them or for them for period of time?

A very wise and good man, Earl Coleman, who has also been a helpful confidante and counselor, said to me recently, "When you let go of your past, your past finally lets go of you."

That is exactly what happened. I have let go. Today, I would prefer that people like me, but if they don't, that's okay. Everyone didn't like Jesus so I certainly cannot expect everyone to like me. *The disciple [student] is not above his master, nor the servant above his lord* (Matthew 10:24). I no longer have that need to seek love from others at any cost. However, I am a caring person by nature and desire friendship with others. My daughter pointed out to me that our family is that way, and it could also have been a trait I learned from my grandmother. My grandmother was the most loving person I've ever known. She was the first to teach me unconditional love. My daughter is right. We learn what we live.

Summary and Reflection

Lord, thou hast heard the desire of the humble: Thou wilt prepare their heart, thou wilt cause thine ear to hear (Psalms 10:17).

For verily I say unto you, That many prophets and righteous men have desired to see those things which ye see, and have not seen them; and to hear those things which ye hear, and have not heard them (Matthew 13:17).

They are of the world: therefore speak they of the world and the world heareth them. We are of God: he that knoweth God heareth us; he that is not of God heareth not us. Hereby know we the spirit of truth, and the spirit of error. Beloved, let us love one another: for love is of God; and every one that loveth is born of God and knoweth God (1 John 4:5-7).

1. Listen closely and hear God's still small voice.
2. Take one hour to be with your Creator, your Master, your Savior, and become His child.

Chapter 11
Fear of Failure and Success

Fear? "I don't have the sin of fear," you may say. Really?

Do you feel inferior to others?

Do you lack self-esteem?

Are you easily intimidated?

Do you feel that everyone is more intelligent, more beautiful, handsome, friendly, capable, etc.?

Do you feel that everyone is looking at you and judging you?

Do you have to be louder than anyone else and stand out, or quieter so as to not be seen?

That, my dear brother or sister, is the sin of fear! That fear may be protecting us from feeling the worthlessness or inferiority that is emanating from all of those unhealed wounds. It may be protecting you from what you feel is rejection. It has become your protection device and your copout. If you feel that you are unworthy of anything:

- *Intellect* (I've never been smart) Everyone else has it easier. I can't continue my education because I don't have _____ (fill in the blank with any excuse);
- *Living a healthy life* (This is me and it's who I'll always be.);
- *Taking a chance on a better life* (He/she won't hire me anyway, so why try, or I can't go back to school);
- *Stepping out in faith* (I never could do anything right. God's not calling me);

- *Taking an interest in our appearance* (Who cares? No one thinks I look good, no matter what I do);
- *Cleaning our homes, spaces, vehicles* (It's no one's business but mine. All I did was clean when I was young; I'm not doing it now).

These all stem from fear of failure and fear of success. I won't try because "if" I fail, someone will criticize me. If I don't try no one will ever know I can't do it, or I don't want to do it, or I'm just too lazy to do it.

Before I go on, I want you to think about who gave you your intellect. It wasn't your mom and dad. God gave it to you. If God gave it to you, there is no limit to what you can learn and do. Even if you're challenged in some way, or just think you are, there are things you can learn that are beyond what you currently understand.

Albert Einstein was diagnosed with ADD and yet in later life he always gave credit to God for his abilities. He was even called the "slow learner" in German.

Now, *stepping out in faith* is another matter. That's just plain scary! I don't believe I have been afraid to step out in faith very often. (We all have different hang-ups.) When I believed God wanted me to move somewhere strange or different, I did it! Sometimes I really didn't want to.

I did not want to move where I am now, and the first few years were miserable for me and all of those around me. It was because I resisted God's will. I wanted my way! I wanted to stay by my Raggedy I friend, Georgia. But I love it here now. The humidity and ice storms leave quite a bit to be desired, but it's okay. I make it through with warm heat in the winter and air conditioning during the summer. Besides, I would never have found my church and my pastor if I hadn't moved here to North Carolina.

There is nothing that compares with being a part of a close and strong body of believers. God always gives us a choice and we have free will. I have been blessed in my life whenever I have followed God's leading. Remember, if God asks us to do something and we choose not to, He will always find someone else to use. His plans are not dependent on any single one of us. Although He delights in our obedience.

The last thing I listed was a *clean home*. Many years ago, someone told me that God will give you only what you can understand. If you cannot understand where you currently live, praise God for it and be proud of it, God will not bless you with something better until you understand where you are.

When my children were young, I told them, "Thank God for dirty dishes, because you know you have food and loved ones to eat with you. Thank God when you do the laundry. You have clothes. And thank God when you clean your home. There are people living in cardboard boxes with dirt floors, and worse."

I remember recently when I attended a state-sponsored training, the majority of the people in the room were younger and seemed more physically fit. Immediately pride and fear came sneaking back in and said "You're not good enough. They're probably all wondering what you're doing this line of work. You aren't as intelligent as they are." I asked the Lord to forgive me for my pride and asked Him to help me to feel equal to others whom I thought were intelligent. I didn't notice until later but suddenly it wasn't important anymore. The stinking thinking just left my mind. I was too busy to entertain nonsense from the devil.

Later in the day, we took a welcome break and walked out onto the patio. Two young women said to me, "You need to come and work with us. We were listening to your comments, and you sound like you really care about people." I immediately praised the Lord.

That same day a young gentleman asked if I lived near a particular area. I told him that I lived quite far from that area and he said if I ever decided to move, I could come to work at his agency. I didn't ask him why he said that. I just praised the Lord.

Once again, the fear tried to stop me from what God had ordained me to do. I have a master's degree and worked hard for it, b-u-t "I" have to realize I am an intelligent creation of my God. Putting on a kangaroo suit doesn't make me a kangaroo. Neither does getting degrees make you more intelligent. The old garbage tapes are still replaying, telling you how dense you are and that you've just got everyone fooled. Well, everyone doesn't fool that easily. If you don't know something, acting like it won't prove anything. But I also care for God's children and it shows, and that was the particular thing that stood out to those who gave me such nice comments.

When we get our thoughts off of ourselves and onto God's other kids, fear doesn't have a chance. God wants us to help others. Many of those you have helped or who have helped you over the years may have been angels. Scripture says that some have entertained angels unaware, and I believe I have entertained many in my lifetime (Hebrews 13:2).

There have been too many times when someone entered my life precisely when I needed help the most; when the event was over, I never saw them again. I definitely believe that our precious Lord has legions of angels at His command who come to our defense, protecting us for His purposes. Often they are there to encourage us and to lead us in a direction we had chosen not to take. Remember also that God has led others into our lives that He wants us to minister to. God has a path for each of us to follow, for our ultimate good and for His divine purposes. Those are the paths that will bring about happiness.

One time when my children were in their early teens, we had all retired to bed for the night. My bed faced my bedroom doorway and down the hall, I could see past the linen closet, the main bath, my daughter's room, and to my mother's room. I awoke in the middle of the night to a bright light shining in my face.

The light was coming from my daughter's room and startled me for a second. I saw the most beautiful person that I have ever seen. I don't know if the angel was male or female. The colors were different from anything I have ever seen on earth, just pure radiance bursting forth. The angel was enormous. Even with our eight-foot ceilings, this person was bent in order to look into my daughter's room.

"Are you an angel?" As soon as I thought it, the answer came to my mind,

"Yes." I wanted to get up and just touch the angel. The angel looked at me and again said, "Things of earth cannot touch the things of heaven." The angel said to my spirit, "Your house will always be blessed," and then disappeared.

The following morning I was in my kitchen speaking to my mother very softly, relaying what had happened during the night. Suddenly my two daughters bolted, running down the hall, across the living room and dining room and began shouting, "Mama, there was a huge angel in our room last night." They both had seen it. My mother and I were speechless as we asked them to describe it. The only thing they could explain was that the angel was large and beautiful with colors they couldn't explain.

I have never forgotten the angel, and neither have my children. In spite of not feeling blessed at times, I can truly say that my family and I have always been blessed in what mattered. We have gone through many struggles but as the scripture says, *I have been young, and now am old, yet have I not seen the righteous forsaken, or His seed begging bread* (Psalms 37:25). We may not have had all the luxuries, but our needs have been met in many strange ways.

Ask your Father to forgive your sin of pride, low self-esteem, or fear. Ask Him to dig it out by its deepest, ugliest roots. Take responsibility for it. Tell Him that you're sorry that you ever invited it into your life. His grace is sufficient for you, according to 2 Corinthians 12:9. Praise the Lord!

Summary and Reflection

Look at areas of your life where pride may have gotten in and taken hold. Is there an area you make excuses for in order to avoid changing something? Is there an area of shame that you hold onto? Is there an area that you even attempt to hide from God?

Bring it out to Him and free yourself from pride. Don't get comfortable with sin. Sin will destroy you.

- Let go of resentments and the need to strike back.
- Let go of the past and get on with what God intends for your life.
- Surrender yourself to God and give up your need to retaliate, even if it's only getting even with yourself. (Which could be the worst form of revenge.)
- Recover the power that God gave you, in Him, when He formed you.
- Stop blaming anyone, even yourself.
- You no longer need attention, sympathy, justification, or secondary gain.
- You no longer need the illusion of power and control over those who hurt you. It is between God and them. They are responsible to God for their actions. You have no responsibility for the actions of anyone other than yourself.

Make a list of all the ways you may act out the sin of pride. An example: I just did it in writing this. My thoughts said, "No one will ever benefit from this. Why write it?" That was my sin of pride. If *I* don't believe it's perfect, I would rather not do it.

Of course, this isn't perfect. Nothing I ever do will be perfect. Only God is perfect. This is simply my humble, human attempt to bring others to forgiving themselves by forgiving others. God can teach us only through example. His death was the ultimate example of forgiveness. In forgiving others, we begin to learn to forgive ourselves, and that will be the hardest thing you will ever do.

Chapter 12
God doesn't settle for second-best. He really doesn't!

For we are his workmanship, created in Christ Jesus unto good works, which God hath before ordained that we should walk in them (Ephesians 2:10).

We were created in His likeness. We are beautifully and wonderfully made. Can any human create anything as beautiful and wondrous as God has created? Think of all the different faces and bodies created since time's beginning, each one unique but made in His likeness. Amazing! No matter that one may be disabled or disfigured (Exodus 4:10-11). We are all beautiful! How could we not be beautiful when we were created by a loving Father who wanted us to resemble Him?

I see parents of newborns always excited when someone tells them that their baby looks just like them. How proud God must feel when someone says we resemble Him in our actions. We should stand with our heads held high because He is our Father. Short, tall, thin, wide, brown, white, black, red, or yellow—or any shade in between or combined—blonde, brunette, redhead, black hair, white hair, curly hair, straight hair, no hair. We all resemble our precious Creator. God loves us because we are His kids. *So God created man in His own image* (Genesis 1:27a).

He wrote us the most incredible love letter—the Bible. The Bible is His personal message and expression of genuine acceptance, caring, and heartfelt love to each of us. He tells us in the Bible that He desires to reach each of us and to let us know of His unfailing love and total acceptance. He wants us! If no one ever wanted you in your life, know that God wants you more than anyone ever will!

God knows about all the pain you've experienced as a result of what others have done or of your own actions. He has entered into that pain with you each step of the way.

He's felt your pain.

He has cried with you and comforted you.

His heart was broken each time you were hurt.

His heart hurts every time you berate yourself in any way.

He made you so perfect, and He watches and listens as we tell ourselves or others that we are not worthy. We tell others that He did not do well in creating us, or others tell us that God did not do well in creating us. They tell us that we're too short, too tall, too ugly, too dark, too light, not the "right" race or from the right breeding. We may suffer a disability of some sort, or we may have a child suffering.

God knows!

He knew from the beginning, and in His sight we are all perfect! Don't let anyone say those things to you, and don't entertain it for a second. We all have the same Father and every one of us looks just like Him. We were created in His likeness! Praise God! His love, compassion, and patience have no end. He is not human. He does not give us three strikes and we're out. He waits for eternity for us to acknowledge Him and love Him and tell Him that He has done a good and perfect work.

Each of us has a unique talent that God has given us for a special mission while we are here. Whether it is the gift of teaching, caring, cleaning, helping, preaching, giving, or giving another compassion. Our gift may also be to teach others compassion. It is a gift we are to use. We are to use it to bring others to Him. Our goal is always to see others saved and whole. His message to us was to go out into the world, teaching the gospel of Jesus Christ and

His salvation. Can you see the talent in your life? Are you using the special gift He has given you? Seek those gifts for yourself.

Summary and Reflection

Make a list of any talents or gifts that you believe the Lord has given you, whether you are using them or not. **Do not rush through this or take it lightly.** Continue to add to the list any time the Lord brings a talent or gift to your remembrance. Begin looking at it. Ask family and friends what gifts they believe you have. You will probably be very surprised.

Then begin working those gifts. Don't put them away and hide them. Bring them out! There is a reason God chose to give them to you. Don't worry about being unworthy, because I can guarantee that you truly are unworthy without the precious gift of Jesus Christ. Don't fall back into that sin of pride but display your gifts and talents. We all need your gifts. The Church needs your gifts. The world needs your gifts. Celebrate those gifts, and then begin ministering!

Chapter 13
Abuse, Addiction, and Recovery

I have heard some counselors tell clients that it might be good for them to confront their abusers. This is just a Raggedy opinion, but I do not believe it's good to go back and confront someone who has abused you. To begin with, you are setting yourself up to feel it all again, all the emotions that you felt at the time the abuse took place and the aftermath following the abuse.

You might also be placing yourself in danger and that is not empowering. It could be a self-defeating act, psychologically, emotionally, and perhaps physically. I do not want to recollect the memories of abuse that I suffered. To take a clue from the one who created all, *As far as the east is from the west, so far hath he removed our transgressions [sins] from us* (Psalms 103:12).

That doesn't mean the abuser's sin is gone, unless they have truly repented and gone to the foot of the Cross and asked forgiveness. It also means that you or I will not choose to recall, dwell on, and recapture the abuse. We must choose not to give it power again. It hurts too much to relive it. It's one of those things that cause us to feel like we are less than others again. It brings back depression and unforgiveness and guilt. It takes our current power away and we are again reduced to an emotional garbage heap.

Many times, we are called to go back and face our abusers. If God calls us to do that, it will be when we are spiritually mature enough to handle it in His love. He will always provide a safe way for us to confront—perhaps with a pastor or with the police or someone in authority to protect us, but never alone.

Perhaps He wants us to speak out in order to witness to that person or to save others from future abuse. God does call the truth to be heard. He does not want any abuser to continue in their ways. He does not want any child hurt. God does not hide things under the rug. He wants sin brought out for healing for all. Abuse isn't only sexual; there are many forms of abuse: emotional, mental, spiritual, and physical. It can even be overindulgence in a child's life, by giving into anything they want or showering them with gifts. God's ultimate plan and desire is to heal every person, and that includes the abuser.

There are many things that God has designed for our good that we abuse. We become addicted to those pleasures and turn them into sin rather than good. Often they are sexual, but there are many others. There are addictions for anything we can think of: legal and illegal drugs, shopping, gambling, talking, gossiping, dieting, eating, exercising, traveling, lying, having people around, cleaning, sleeping, stealing, etc.

I worked for a Native American tribal agency for a short period doing alcohol and drug counseling. I would observe those coming in with their addictions and think to myself, *that is me*. Perhaps not with the same practicing addiction at that time, but I was addicted to something. The need, the cravings, the withdrawal, they're all there within us. We just judge others more harshly than ourselves. We may not like their addiction, but ours is no prettier and no less sinful.

There is no degree of sin in God's eyes. We just prefer to think we are a little better than "those" people. There is no difference in my addiction to work than the I.V. drug user's addiction to the needle. I need to work to bring about a good feeling in myself. I need my house clean. It pleases me. It releases bottled-up tensions within my body and frees me at the end of the day when I can say I did a good job or I can look at a well-ordered home. The I.V.

drug user has the same feelings. It frees them when they feel the drug entering their body. The tension, built up by the need, is released and the chemical, at that moment in time, is their salvation.

I have been a recovering addict and alcoholic for the last 39 years. I was addicted to stimulants and to alcohol and I can still recall the need I had for those stimulants. I would feel tired from working or doing whatever I was doing. Actually, I never needed an excuse. The first time I tried stimulants, I was hooked. I didn't know I was an addict at the time. A kind-hearted doctor gave me a few amphetamines to help me get through my day, but it didn't take me long to get out on the streets and buy them illegally.

I was divorced at the time and working one full-time and two part-time jobs, in addition to raising three children. The drugs sure helped me get through my days and even my nights. I found I didn't really need to sleep much and I sure didn't need to eat. I thought it was wonderful! All I had to do was swallow the pills and drink some alcohol.

I found any reason to feed my addiction. If one pill worked, I took ten or twenty to make sure they really worked. I was not aware of my irrational behavior. I cleaned constantly, day and night, and couldn't stop talking. With the alcohol and drugs combined, I'm not sure how I lived through it.

It was the grace of God that saved my life. It never occurred to me then that He had a purpose for me. I loved the taste of alcohol and it fed everything my brain seemed to need. I never drank socially, though. I drank to consume as much as I could. I had no tolerance for it. I could never stop at one or two social drinks, it was all consuming. If I knew there was alcohol in the world, I wanted it and usually had it. I functioned through my addiction, and many people were not even aware that I was an addict—or they may have known and been afraid to confront me with it.

I probably would not have listened to them at that time anyway, or I would have become angry. I am no longer a practicing addict but will always be in recovery. I can never permit myself to taste alcohol or use any stimulant drug again. Whenever I have gone to a new physician, one of the first things I tell the physician is to never give me narcotics or anything with alcohol in it. I explain to them that even if I beg and plead, do not give it to me. I believe that God can and will deliver us from anything but I also believe there is a physical price to pay for my sin. We must always wear our work shoes in this life. Working on staying away from addictions is a primary step.

God created certain medications to be used to aid in the healing of our bodies. He did not give me drugs to abuse or use recreationally. I chose to do that. It was a conscious choice I made. Again, free will enters the picture. Today I have allergies to so many drugs and will always wonder if my addictions brought about my allergies. It makes no difference any longer because I know that my God will always take care of me.

Are you wondering why and how I quit my chemical addictions? All addicts will eventually hit a bottom and that was mine. I was drinking when I slapped my four-year-old son in the face. I had vowed not to hit my children, but here I was drunk and my beautiful son was asking me to play with him. I asked him several times not to bother me, and then I hit him. Not just a slap, but a backhanded slap across his face. The shock in his face was enough for me. How can the same hand that had shown him love also cause him such pain? My action broke my heart and still lives with me today. I have deep regret over that incident.

I did end up in the hospital because of withdrawal. Our bodies become adjusted to certain chemicals that we abuse and when we try to stop, the body and brain scream out in anger. Praise the Lord for His deliverance. The addictive part of me will always be there. I created it within myself but I no longer have to indulge. It has no power over me by the grace of Jesus Christ and His power.

Many people, and Christians especially, think of addiction as solely as drugs and alcohol. People experience addictions of all types. There are addictions to cleaning, shopping, overeating, gambling, sex, money, television, gossip, exercise and playing games. We even had one woman recently on the news addicted to bearing children.

Those seem to be the more acceptable addictions, but addictions they are.

You may be experiencing one of these addictions, but not claiming it or thinking of it as an addiction. Anything that takes our eyes off what God has planned for us and consumes our time can be an addiction. It can be difficult breaking an addiction, but it can be even more difficult becoming aware that you have one. We need to ask God to show us our addictions and make them clear to us; then don't dismiss what He shows you. My daughter recently said that if someone cannot quit their addictions, they can try to fast their addictions. I had to think about that, and it made perfect sense. If you are not ready to quit whatever addiction you have, try to fast it unto the Lord. If you're a shopping addict, try to go shopping one time and purchase absolutely nothing. Tell the Lord you are doing it as a fast unto Him. He will bless your heart to please Him.

Summary and Reflection

Spend some time thinking about the times you've judged someone who you assumed or knew was an addict. I mean addicted to drugs or alcohol—or perhaps even sex.

Have you ever considered yourself as an addict? There are so many things that we can easily become addicted to without realizing it. Addiction to shopping is an exciting addiction for most females and some males. Sports, image, professions, health, vitamins, television, internet, food, cleaning, competition, gambling, possessions, can all become addictions.

Anything can become an addiction. Can you judge another's addiction when you also suffer from addictions? Is your addiction healthier? Does your addiction bring you closer to God or farther away from Him? As long as our addictions are legal, we cannot see the harm in them, but anything that takes our time and focus from God is sin.

In your journal or notebook, make a list of any and all addictions you feel you may have. No one else need ever see your list. Then offer your list to God and ask Him to help you work through them. Ask Him to break your addictions. Then ask Him to forgive you for the times you've judged another with an addiction.

Chapter 14
Mistakes We Make as Parents

Before I go further, I need to tell you about the time I apologized to my children for raising them in church. (Please continue reading before you judge that statement.)

I always kept them in church as much as possible, and I still believe that if children are reared with the ways of the Lord, even if they leave for a time, they will come back. Does that sound familiar? It should, if you know the Word of God at all. The Word says, *Train up a child in the way he should go: and when he is old, he will not depart from it* (Proverbs 22:6). If God says it, it's the truth!

My children were taught to trust their Christian brothers and sisters. I tried to keep anyone whom I felt was not Christ-like away from them. They were raised to trust people. Can you see where the problem would be when they were grown and out in the world? They trusted everyone! And people lied to them and hurt them. They were shocked when it happened repeatedly and would say to me "But Mom, so-and-so promised" or "So-and-so said it was the truth."

The poor babies didn't know how to act in the world. That was when I had to apologize for raising them with good Christian people and never thinking to tell them that everyone was not like the people they were used to. True Christians are accountable to God. If a person doesn't believe in God, then who is he accountable to?

Himself?

Who else could he or she be accountable to? Isn't that a scary thought? My children dated and believed what their boyfriends or girlfriends said to them. Explain to your children the way the world is without a true commitment to

Jesus Christ. Warn your children and keep warning them. Keep them safe and close to the Lord. Non-Christian friends will lie to them about drugs and so many other things. The Words says to put on the full armor of God.

Put on the whole armour of God, that ye may be able to stand against the wiles of the devil. For we wrestle not against flesh and blood, but against principalities, against powers, against the rulers of the darkness of this world, against spiritual wickedness in high places. Wherefore take unto you the whole armour of God, that ye may be able to withstand in the evil day, and having done all, to stand. Stand therefore, having your loins girt about with truth and having on the breastplate of righteousness: And your feet shod with the preparation of the gospel of peace; Above all, taking the shield of faith, wherewith ye shall be able to quench all the fiery darts of the wicked. And take the helmet of salvation, and the sword of the Spirit, which is the word of God: Praying always with prayer and supplication in the Spirit, and watching thereunto with all perseverance and supplication for all saints (Ephesians 6:11-18).

Make sure your children are wearing that armor, and make sure that yours fits well, too. You can easily lose armor that is too small or large for you, and one not applied properly can fall off when the enemy tries to tempt you or attacks.

When I said to make sure your children wear the full armor of God, I'm not just talking about the world apart from the Church. We need to teach them about having a personal relationship with Jesus Christ and not just going through the actions of attending church. We need to teach our children to be intimate with Jesus to prepare them for the world, whether in or out of church. Don't forbid certain music because it's not of the Lord, but teach through the Word why it's important to draw closer to the Lord.

If they are prepared when the things of the world are around and your children are on their own, they can rely on Christ and the Word. They need to know how to stand in their faith even when no other Christian is around, or they will be swayed by everything that comes at them.

We, as parents, try to do everything for our children. We tell them what to do, what to listen to, who to hang around with, where to go, and even what to eat without first teaching them to have that personal relationship so they can depend on Christ no matter what.

Just telling a child to do something because it is in the Bible isn't enough. We wish it were, and so does God, but it isn't. Don't do for your children because they won't learn to do for themselves with Jesus. They need to know Who their Source is and Who they can always depend on. We, as parents, will not always be with them, but God will always be there for them.

Often we insist that our children have only Christian friends, but sometimes those friends are worse than the youth who have never attended church or come to a saving knowledge of Jesus Christ. If our children are not permitted non-Christian friends, who will witness to those youth who have never had the opportunity to hear the Word?

We and our children are not called to sit in pews and witness to each other. We are called to witness to all corners of the world, and that includes other youth. Get up and get out of those pews! You weren't saved or called to just sit on your backside!

You cannot force a relationship between your children and the Lord. Sometimes you have to permit them to make their own mistakes and learn from them. That's the time to pray continuously for them.

Lead them by your example. If your children observe you cheating, lying, swearing, or stealing, what will they learn? They certainly won't learn to seek the Lord. Children have a hard time believing that what their parents do is wrong. If you always lead them in a Godly manner, they will eventually learn to seek the Lord first and foremost.

My eldest grandson was recently listening to a certain rock musician that I had trouble with when my children were young. But my grandson enjoys rock music. I would have preferred almost any other artist, but my grandson liked this particular one. My daughter did not forbid him to listen to the worldly music but instead filled her home with Christian rock music. My grandson told me yesterday that he's thrown out all of CDs by that other artist just because he was tired of them.

He's really enjoying Christian rock now, and it's all he wants to listen to. I was concerned when my daughter permitted him to listen to the worldly rock music, but I've since learned that she's pretty smart and follows the Lord's leading instead of mine. I will be eternally grateful for that. I may give wrong advice, but the Lord never does.

My youngest grandson had decided that he no longer believed in God because He couldn't see Him or hear Him. My daughter told him he could believe that if he could give her just one piece of proof that God did not exist. After one week, he did not succeed.

My daughter pointed to the vase on her entertainment center and asked if he could see who created the vase. He said, "No." My daughter shared with him that even though he could not see the person, he knew they existed. He said he did, but he still did not believe there is a God. His mother shared with him the trees outside and all of nature were created by God, even though he couldn't see Him. She said it was the same as not being able to see the creator of the vase but believing that someone created it.

At that time he held a passion for skateboarding. While out skateboarding a few weeks after the conversation with his mother, he suffered a terrible accident. His foot turned completely backwards. The physicians feared that he could lose his foot due to the extensive damage. He spent six months with his foot elevated, not knowing the entire time whether he would be able to keep his foot or not.

That was when he began praying to God, the One he never believed in prior to his accident. He did not lose his foot. The physician told him that only God could have saved his foot. He still walks with a limp and his foot slightly turned, but he will tell anyone that he definitely believes in God. Often he will call and tell me that he is praying for me and his Papa. None of us was prepared for what happened to him, but we're amazed how the Lord was able to teach Micah through this that He is always there, waiting for us to reach out and accept Him.

Since that time, Micah has told everyone how God showed Himself to him. Micah now goes through daily life armed with the Lord.

Teach your children what the whole armor of God is daily: covering themselves with the Blood of Jesus Christ, with God's truth, His righteousness, His faith, His peace, reading their Bible, and being in prayer for themselves and for others.

Summary and Reflection

We as parents often quote the scriptures to our children of how God tells them to obey His rules. We, however, often forget the rules our Father gave us for raising our children.

Verily I say unto you, Except ye be converted and become as little children, ye shall not enter into the kingdom of heaven. Whosoever therefore shall humble himself as this little child, is greatest in the kingdom of heaven. And whoso shall receive one such little child in my name receiveth me (Matthew 18:3-5).

And ye fathers, provoke not your children to wrath: but bring them up in the nurture and admonition of the Lord (Ephesians 6:4).

Fathers, provoke not your children to anger, lest they be discouraged (Colossians 3:21).

1. Do your children see you reading the Scriptures?
2. Do your children see you praying for yourself, for them, and for others?
3. Do your children see an example of forgiveness in you?
4. Do your children see you standing in faith, no matter what is taking place?
5. Do your children see you attempting to excuse your own bad behavior?
6. Do you compliment or verbally tear down your children? Do you tell them and show them how important they are to you and the Lord?
7. Do you take the time to sit with your children and discuss how important it is for them to arm themselves daily with the Lord's armor and protection, even when it might not be comfortable for you to do so?
8. Do your children hear you gossip or talk badly of others?

9.   Do you excuse their bad behavior to others or make them accountable for their actions?

10. Do you listen to your children talk without judgment and without interrupting?

Chapter 15
Blaming God

People place blame on God when they harbor unforgiveness in their souls. Often through the illness of self or loved ones, or death, they become angry with God and no longer choose to believe His promises or look to His plan. They say "If God is a loving god, why did He do this, or permit this?" They fail to look at the free will we were given that often causes problems. We might hear on the news about a drunk driver who killed an innocent victim. Often the intoxicated driver will escape harm God is still attempting to save them.

I had a wonderful great-aunt and great-uncle who were killed by a drunk driver. He suffered only a few bruises. I was angry with God for permitting it to happen. My uncle and aunt were innocent victims, and it was not God's will for them to die an early death. It is not God's will that children are abused or are killed in traffic accidents or through birth or illness. It is not God's will that a father or mother be taken from their children through death.

I do know that if God had taken the drunk's free will away, He would have had to take free will from each and every one of us. None of us would have it, and we would indeed become robots.

God does not respect one person more highly than another. He deals with each of us equally, never failing in His Word. Neither can God give us the complete freedom that we often desire. To give one person total freedom would mean taking the freedom from every other person.

What if I had that total freedom and decided that I wanted to drive 120 miles an hour down the main street near my home? That would be taking the freedom from every person on that road, and even their families. Surely I would kill and maim several people in my freedom.

Instead, God loves us so much that He makes us accountable. We are held accountable for every action we take, and that accountability should bring us joy. Being accountable brings us joy because we know what we are doing is the good and perfect will of God. It will bring us peace, joy, and harmony.

Judging ourselves by others' outward appearance

I remember a woman I knew who always appeared to be blessed, materially and in every way. She had a beautiful home, expensive vehicles, and always took exciting vacations. But she was a nasty lady.

You all have known someone like her. They appear righteous on the outside, but we often don't know what goes on at home. I have heard that if we treated our friends the way we treat our family, we wouldn't have any friends. That was her. She would talk badly about others, screaming and yelling at people. She did things that just weren't very nice. She cheated anyone she could. Her husband was an elder in the church and she was a deaconess. They gave much to the church, so they were always used as an example of how God would bless us if we gave. Looking at her outwardly, one would think she had a wonderful heart. She could be seen as an example of how we should be living, but when you got into her inner circle you saw the truth. She was attempting to buy her way into Heaven without having to live an actual Godly life. The amazing part was is she always believed she was living a Godly life.

Reminiscent of Jacob and Esau, Genesis 25 through 31. They can look good on the outside, as when Jacob put the fur on to fool his father, but on the inside they aren't very nice. God blessed Jacob because He had given a promise to Jacob's father, Isaac, that Jacob's descendants would prosper. God doesn't break His promises, so He fulfilled what He set out to do in Jacob. Many who claim to be Christians can be conniving and look for outward glory.

One day while visiting this woman, I witnessed her screaming at an elderly person who was staying in her home. Later, I was driving on the Interstate by myself, crying my poor little heart out to God. I was imagining myself as such a nice person and a good Christian, and here was this nasty lady seeming to be blessed. I was literally screaming, "Why are you blessing her? She's a rotten lady! I'm a good person and you aren't blessing me as much as you've blessed her." I was in fact judging her—which is God's job, not mine, He knows the heart.

Was I acting like a good Christian? No way! I was behaving like a spoiled brat, jealous of someone who had more toys than I had. After about fifteen or twenty minutes of my tears and yelling to God, I heard this small, still voice in my heart, "Malachi chapter 3." At first I just ignored it, thinking to myself, "What is that about?" But it kept coming to my mind and finally got my attention. When I arrived home, I grabbed my Bible and read Malachi 3. Have you ever read it, I mean really read it? I was completely shocked. God had heard me and He wasn't having any of my whiny baby crying.

Malachi 3 reads: *Behold, I will send my messenger, and he shall prepare the way before me: and the Lord, whom ye seek, shall suddenly come to his temple, even the messenger of the covenant, whom ye delight in: behold, he shall come, saith the Lord of hosts. But who may abide the day of his coming? And who shall stand when he appeareth? For he is like a refiner's fire, and like fullers' soap: And he shall sit as a refiner and purifier of silver: and he shall purify the sons of Levi, and purge them as gold and silver, that they may offer unto the Lord an offering in righteousness, Then shall the offering of Judah and*

*Jerusalem be pleasant unto the Lord, as in the days of old,
and as in former years. And I will come near to you to
judgment; and I will be a swift witness against the
sorcerers, and against the adulterers, and against false
swearers, and against those that oppress the hireling in his
wages, the widow, and the fatherless, and that turn aside
the stranger from his right, and fear not me, saith the Lord
of hosts. For I am the Lord, I change not; therefore ye sons
of Jacob are not consumed. Even from the days of your
fathers ye are gone away from mine ordinances, and have
not kept them. Return unto me, and I will return unto you,
saith the Lord of hosts. But ye said, Wherein shall we
return? Will a man rob God? Yet ye have robbed me. But
ye say, Wherein have we robbed thee? In tithes and
offerings. Ye are cursed with a curse: for ye have robbed
me, even this whole nation. Bring ye all the tithes into the
storehouse, that there may be meat in mine house, and
prove me now herewith, saith the Lord of hosts, if I will not
open you and the windows of heaven, and pour you out a
blessings, that there shall not be room enough to receive it.
And I will rebuke the devourer for your sakes, and he shall
not destroy the fruits of your ground; neither shall you vine
cast her fruit before the time in the field, saith the Lord of
hosts. And all nations shall call you blessed: for ye shall be
a delightsome land, saith the Lord of hosts. Your words
have been stout against me, saith the Lord. Yet ye say,
What have we spoken so much against thee? Ye have said,
It is vain to serve God: and what profit is it that we have
kept his ordinance, and that we have walked mournfully
before the Lord of hosts? And now we call the proud
happy; yea, they that work wickedness are set up; yea, they
that tempt God are even delivered. Then they that feared
the Lord spake often one to another: and the Lord
hearkened, and heard it, and a book of remembrance was
written before him for them that feared the Lord, and that
thought upon his name. And they shall be mine, saith the*

Lord of hosts, in that day when I make up my jewels, and I will spare them, as a man spareth his own son that serveth him. Then shall ye return, and discern between the righteous and the wicked, between him that serveth God and him that serveth him not (Malachi 3).

I want to tell you the end of the story. She divorced her husband when he was near death, leaving him penniless. She did marry the wealthier widower, and he was dead within two years. Yes, she had a lot of material possessions, but she was never really blessed. She was never at peace or happy. Nothing, no matter how much, made her happy.

I was amazed at Malachi 3. I couldn't even talk or pray for a while. I just went into shock. God really did hear me! God really did speak to me! But then I thought, *I better get busy telling Him I'm sorry and asking forgiveness.* He was telling me that I was not the one to judge the wicked. That was His job, and He would take care of it when the time was right. Once again, my mouth had gotten far beyond my spirit, and nasty, selfish thoughts were in me and out of my mouth. I was judging someone else, and my sin was even greater. All I really thought about was myself and my hurt feelings and my jealousy of her always seeming to be blessed. God showed me her sin was not mine to judge, but I was sinning through judging her.

A young friend in Oregon, Natalie, is Raggedy I's granddaughter. I love her dearly. She sent me this dialogue in an email recently. -It is an urban legend, but it conveys a great point.

An atheist professor of philosophy was speaking to his class on the problem science has with God. He asked one of his new students to stand and began questioning him.

Professor: "You are a Christian, aren't you?"
Student: "Absolutely, sir."

"So you believe in God?"

"Absolutely!"

"Is God good?"

"Absolutely, sir."

"Is God all-powerful?"

"Yes, sir," said the student.

"My brother died of cancer even though he prayed to God to heal him. Most of us would attempt to help others who are ill. But God didn't. How is this God good then?"

Silence from the student.

"You can't answer, can you? Let's start again. Is God good?"

"Yes," said the student.

"Is satan good?"

"No."

"Where does satan come from?" asked the professor.

"From God."

"That's right. Tell me, is there evil in this world?"

"Yes."

"Evil is everywhere, isn't it? And God did make everything? Correct?"

"Yes."

"So who created evil?" asked the professor.

Silence, again from the student.

"Is there sickness? Is there immorality? Hatred? Ugliness? All these terrible things exist in the world, don't they?"

"Yes, sir," said the student

"So, who created them?"

Silence from the student

"Science says you have five senses you use to identify and observe the world around you. Tell me, have you ever seen God?"

"No sir."

"Have you ever heard God?

126

"No sir."

"Have you ever felt your God, tasted your God, smelled your God? Have you ever had any sensory perception of God for that matter?"

"No sir. I'm afraid I haven't," said the student.

"Yet you still believe in Him?"

"Yes sir."

"According to empirical, testable, demonstrable protocol, science says your God doesn't exist. What do you say to that?"

"Nothing. I only have my faith."

"Yes, faith. And that is the problem science has."

"Is there such a thing as cold?" asked the student.

"Yes," said the professor.

"No sir, there isn't."

The lecture theater becomes silent.

"Sir, you can have lots of heat, even more heat, superheat, mega heat, white heat, a little heat or no heat, but we don't have anything called cold. We can hit 458 degrees below zero, which is no heat, but we can't go any further after that. There is no such thing as cold. Cold is only a word we use to describe the absence of heat. We cannot measure cold. Heat is energy. Cold is not the opposite of heat, sir, just the absence of it."

There is pin-drop silence in the lecture theater.

"What about darkness, Professor? Is there such a thing as darkness?"

"Yes. What is night if there isn't darkness?" said the professor.

"You're wrong again, sir. Darkness is the absence of something. You can have low light, normal light, bright light, flashing light, but if you have no light constantly, you have nothing and it's called darkness, isn't it? In reality, darkness isn't. If it were, you would be able to make darkness darker, wouldn't you?"

"So what is the point you are trying to make?"

"Sir, my point is your philosophical premise is flawed. You are working on the premise of duality. You argue there is life and then there is death, a good God and a bad God. You are viewing the concept of God as something finite, something we can measure. Sir, science cannot even explain a thought. It uses electricity and magnetism, but has never been seen, much less fully understood. To view death as the opposite of life is to be ignorant of the fact that death cannot exist as a substantive thing. Death is not the opposite of life, just the absence of it. Now tell me, Professor, do you teach your students that they evolved from a monkey?"

"Of course, I do."

"Have you ever observed evolution with your own eyes, sir?"

"No." He's starting to understand where this conversation is going.

"Since no one has ever observed the process of evolution at work and cannot even prove that this process is an on-going endeavor, are you not teaching your opinion, sir? Are you not a scientist, but a preacher?"

The class laughs.

"Is there anyone in the class who has ever seen or heard the Professor's brain, felt it, touched it, or smelled it? No one appears to have done so. So, according to the established rules of empirical, stable, demonstrable protocol, science says that you have no brain. With all due respect sir, how do we then trust your lectures?"

The room is silent. The professor stares at the student.

"I guess you'll have to take them on faith," said the professor.

"That is it, sir. . .the link between man and God is faith. That is all that keeps things moving and alive."

I thought this dialogue was especially brilliant because of the great lesson it would have taught the professor. My father used to say that part of the problem with the world was too much education. My father was a college graduate and was not putting down academia or the need to further our education. What he was saying was that often people become so educated they feel they don't need God any longer. They seem to grow out of what they knew and now believe to be an immature state. But that is precisely when they need the Lord most in their lives.

Even Albert Einstein said, "Give me God's thoughts. The rest is nonsense." Einstein knew the source of his intelligence. He knew the Source and Beginning of everything in our universe. I cannot understand why someone very intelligent in math or physics would not be able to understand and accept God. Every single thing God created was done with order, intellect, and mathematics.

When my father died at age 54, I was devastated. I could not believe that this kind, loving man would die at such an early age, and I was angry with God for taking him.

We feel that our parents will always be around. We need them. Why would they ever leave us? My father died suddenly. He had gone into his beautiful Japanese garden and picked my mother a fragrant bouquet of flowers after a long day at work. He walked to their door, knocked, presented her with the flowers, and dropped onto the walkway. He died instantly.

When I heard the news, I rushed to the hospital, unbelieving. I thought it was all a mistake. Not my Dad! I saw my poor mother and asked her if it was true. Sobbing, she said, "Yes." I told her I wanted to see him. She took me to where he was. He had a sheet covering him and I pulled it back. I was stunned. My father had the most beautiful smile on his face. It felt like a horrible joke someone was playing on me.

How could he be dead and have that smile? I screamed at the doctor to get the sheet off of him and get him off that bed. I wanted him up. I knew he was alive. The doctor gently assured me that he had passed and that he did, indeed, die with a smile.

The last Saturday of my father's life, he and my mother had taken my children and me to dinner. I had stopped my addictions by that time and my father was so proud of me. At dinner he said, "I know that you've stopped the drugs and the alcohol, but what I want to know is, have you found the Lord?"

I was surprised that my Dad asked me that. I said, "Of course, Dad." Then he smiled and asked me to say the Lord's Prayer. I didn't know why he wanted me to say it right there in the restaurant, but I did.

He said, "Now that's what matters."

He was so pleased and smiled all through dinner. The following Thursday, just two days before he went home to the Lord, he came to visit one evening without my mother. That was very unusual. My mother was agoraphobic and he never left her alone. She was terrified of being anywhere alone. She had to be with someone she trusted. That night, he and I sat on my front steps and he talked to me about his life.

He told me about all the hurts he had endured. He spoke of his mother's flight from Arkansas, taking him with her to escape a cruel and drunken husband. My father had a sister, a year or two younger than he, but I never learned why his mother didn't take her daughter with them.

My father never knew why and never asked. She took my father and escaped to Chicago, trying to begin a new life away from the abuse. My father was young and did not remember his father. We visited his sister once, in Louisiana, when I was about eight or nine years old. My Dad told me that she was living the same as his mother had, poor, hard working in the cotton fields, and abused by her husband.

They had three daughters, my cousins, whom I remember meeting only once. They were sharecroppers on a cotton farm and lived in poverty. His sister knew the Lord, though, and celebrated even the poor life that she had. I said celebrated because she seemed so happy and was not even aware of her lot. She worked hard in the fields and hard at home while raising three beautiful daughters who also knew the Lord. I did speak with my uncle on the telephone before his death, and I believe that he came to know the Lord before my aunt passed away.

My father spoke volumes to me that night and I was sincerely touched. I had never known him to speak about personal matters with anyone, especially me. He must have talked with my mother but certainly with no one else. I asked him why he was telling me all of this, and he said he just wanted me to know that everyone goes through terrible times in life, but the Lord is always there with them.

That night he also asked me if anything ever happened to him, would I take my mother to live with me and be kind to her. Of course, I said I would and remember saying to him, "But Dad, nothing is going to happen to you."

I believe he knew the Lord was calling him home and he was ready to go. He portrayed such a tender picture of God's love to me that night. He, like God, wanted to make sure his child was going to be okay. He also wanted to make sure his bride, my mother, would be all right. That's the same way the Lord protects His bride, the Church. Years later I realized what a powerful message and gift he gave me that night. He tried to live God's Word.

I mentioned that my mother was agoraphobic. Agoraphobia usually results from a severe trauma and many people are incapacitated for life with it. My mother became agoraphobic when I was less than a year old. She was Lebanese and brought up in a traditional Lebanese family that put a high priority on their male children. My grandmother was the most wonderful, loving person I've ever known, but as children there are many things we choose not to see. My grandfather was an alcoholic and practiced it as often as he could. One of his children, my uncle Sam, was also an alcoholic but most likely schizophrenic, too.

Right after I was born, my father was called to the Army. World War II had not quite ended. My brother was eighteen months older than I was, and my mother was still nursing me. The military sent my mother a check every month and my father tried to send her whatever he could. My mother, brother, and I were living with my grandmother, along with my grandfather and my uncle. My uncle demanded every penny my mother received and would not permit her to spend anything.

My father was unaware of what was going on at home. Consequently, when my mother would receive a check from my father, she would walk to the bank and cash it immediately to give to her brother. On her way home she would stop at the butcher shop and buy a piece of pork, the cheapest meat available.

On her way home, she would eat it in order to nourish herself to breastfeed me. She was eating only small amounts or nothing at home because her brother would yell about the expense. Because of the raw pork she ate, she became very ill. Eventually my father was called home from the military because the doctor feared she would die. He realized what happened after speaking with my mother and immediately moved all of us away from her family. Several years later my grandmother had her first heart attack and was very ill. Consequently, my parents decided it was best if we moved back to help in caring for my grandmother.

My mother remained agoraphobic and needed to feel protected by someone she knew loved her and whom she trusted. My Raggedy friend, Georgia (Raggedy I), recently sent me something my mother should have read: "Never let the enemy tell you that you are worthless or insignificant. You have value in the eyes of God so great that it was worth dying for. You are a blessing to the world. You are so precious to God that heaven would not be complete without you." I cried when I first read that, wishing my mother would have known that. She knew the Lord but did not know she was worthy because He loved her so much. It would have been easy for my mother to have blamed God for all the years she suffered with agoraphobia, but she chose instead to be a blessing to everyone she met.

How often have we blamed God for an illness, a tragedy, a loss that has happened in our lives? Have you ever blamed Him? God does not cause negative circumstances or illness. However, He does permit certain things for our and others' growth. An example of this is what happened with my grandson Micah's foot and ankle. God never caused the accident, but He permitted it because He knew that was what would bring Micah to Christ.

When my mother was dying of cancer, I asked her to take pain medication her doctor had prescribed. She would say, "The Lord is sufficient for me." She never took anything but over-the-counter Tylenol. I was amazed she was so strong and didn't even know it.

One night about three weeks before her passing, I heard her in the middle of the night and asked if she was okay. I had placed an intercom between her bedroom and mine. She was sitting in the dining room with her Bible. I asked her if she was alright and she said, "I just had the strangest dream." She was lying on her right side, facing her bedroom windows, when she saw the devil in all his nastiness next to her bed, reaching for her. She became scared and pulled away, turning to her left side to get away, and there stood the Lord in all of His shining glory, holding His hands out to her. She said she felt so comforted.

When my mother was very close to her death, we took her to the hospital. She was there for three days. During that time I made every deal I could with God to save her life. It wasn't her faith that was lacking, it was mine. God wanted her home with Him. I wanted my mother and wasn't listening for God's will. Every morning the nurses would take her down for radiation treatments. My children and I never left her side. I sent them home at night to sleep, but they were back first thing in the morning.

On the third morning I was resting in a chair next to her bed, trying to stay awake, when I heard a male voice call her name. Startled, I looked around, but no one was there. Twice more I heard the voice call her name, and then I knew. The nurses came in shortly after to transport her down for radiation. I told them, "No more!" I had already washed the marks off her body where they had placed X's for the radiation treatments. I told them she was going home today.

They thought I had been there too long and was becoming delirious. I said, "No," and explained that I had heard the Lord call her name. They humored me and let us be. Several times they came in to check on both of us. When my daughters arrived, we washed her body. We didn't want the nurses or anyone to touch her. About three in the afternoon, I was standing by the window and I heard my mother take a breath. With great alarm, I rushed to her side. She had taken her last breath. I was holding her in my arms and it was the first time I had ever felt a spirit leave the body. I felt her spirit rise upwards. It was also the last time I was afraid of dying. I knew where she went. She went home.

The Lord healed her completely that day by taking her to heaven with Him, but He also healed me. He is a good God. I grieved for my loss for years, but I knew I was grieving because I did not have her here with me. As I was grieving, the saints in heaven were celebrating her arrival.

After her death, someone gave me a poem. For over a year after my mother's going home to the Lord, my eldest daughter, Sabrina, would not read the poem and would get up and leave whenever her grandmother was mentioned. She felt so guilty because prior to my mother's death, Sabrina thought if she didn't help her do things, she would be forced to do them herself and consequently get better. She blamed God for taking someone she loved so much for a long time. Before my mother's death, she asked her to forgive her for being mean. She also had to ask God to forgive her for blaming Him. Her grandmother told her she knew why she was doing it and loved her for it. My mother gave her a blessing at that moment.

I am standing on the seashore. A
ship spreads her sails to the morning breeze
and starts for the ocean. I stand watching
her until she fades on the horizon, and
someone at my side says,
  "She is gone."
  "Gone where?"
The loss of sight is in me, not in her.
Just at the moment when someone says,
"She is gone," there are others who are
watching her coming. Other voices take up
the glad shout, "Here she comes." And that
is dying and I will see her there.
  (Author unknown)

I will never know who placed that poem into my hand but will always be grateful for the comfort and witness it brought me. I did not attend my mother's funeral. I could not. She was no longer there. I had taken care of her for eighteen years, never being out of her sight, and felt I could not abandon her earthly body to the grave. I have been to the grave twice to view her headstone, but I know that she is not there. The headstone is a witness to others. It reads, "She was a woman of faith."

Recently in a book I was reading, it said that "Relationships show us who we are. They mirror back to us our own dysfunctional ways. They should serve to wake us to the need for change in our own lives."

The author may not have even been a Christian author; nevertheless, it witnessed to me. The relationships that I had with my father and mother revealed my dysfunctional ways. Both my mother and father showed me that I was not in a close personal relationship of trust with my Savior, Jesus Christ. Neither of them did it deliberately, but their lives showed me how to live in a personal relationship with my Savior. My father passed with a smile, in spite of a massive heart attack. My mother passed in total peace and reliance on the words of her Savior, *We are confident, I say, and willing rather to be absent from the body, and to be present with the Lord.* (2 Corinthians 5:8).

Summary and Reflection

Have you ever blamed God when an illness or calamity came on you? Most of us would say, "Never!" But do we secretly blame Him? Often we wonder why God permitted whatever it was to come upon us. We wonder what we've done wrong to cause it. We never tell others or even admit out loud that God would do this, but it's there nonetheless.

We don't want to speak it aloud because then God would hear it. He hears our innermost thoughts.

*I know that thou canst do everything, and that no thought can be withholden from thee (*Job 42:2).

The Lord knoweth the thoughts of man, that they are vanity (Psalms 94:11).

But sanctify the Lord God in your hearts: and be ready always to give an answer to every man that asketh you a reason of the hope that is in you with meekness and fear (1 Peter 3:15).

List times when you blamed God or tried to hold Him accountable.

Chapter 16
Did anyone ever tell you how much God loves you?

I have seen many Christians so despondent and forlorn that it breaks my heart at times. By nature, I am an observer of people. Often I'll sit back and as I observe others, I can almost feel the hurt in them. It is painful to see and realize that there is nothing you can do. I know one woman in particular who has been heavy on my heart since I first saw her. She is a beautiful woman, very exotic in her natural appearance, but she doesn't know how wonderful she is and how God must celebrate her very existence.

She was instrumental in my beginning this book. I observed her Sunday after Sunday and prayed for her, but the weight would not leave my heart. I still have not spoken to her of the heaviness because it just hasn't been appropriate. I would never want to bring her further pain, but I would love to see her accept healing from the Lord. She would be a mighty witness to others.

The first time I heard her sing in the church choir, she had the voice of an angel. Not the dramatic voice of an operatic soprano, but the voice of one who sings to worship and cry to the Lord. No audience is necessary for her. Her words fly from her soul to God's ears. "Soulful" would be the word to describe her singing. It's a voice that is sung from deep within one's being, crying out supplications and tribute to a holy God. She celebrates the Name of the Most High in song, but humility spills from this woman.

How often I have prayed to the Lord to give me that dignity, not pride in oneself, but dignity in standing before my Lord and Savior with an attitude of humbleness and complete abandon to Him. I am not one to completely abandon myself in others' sight or hearing. I praise my Lord, in song, when I'm alone. I praise Him in prayer in church, but there is just something lacking in my singing voice. I'm sure the angels change my voice before it reaches the heavenly throne, so as not to offend God's ears! I often say that jokingly because I believe God loves to hear each of our voices, no matter how tone-deaf we are.

Often I will hear this small voice say to me, "You have committed the unpardonable sin." That is when I know the devil has gone too far again. He attempts to appear as an angel of light and this catches many in sin. They hear that same small voice tell them:

"It's okay to do what feels right from time to time. You're only human. God knows that you aren't perfect yet."

"He knows that you will never be perfect until you enter His kingdom in heaven."

"You won't be perfect until you die, then God will change you."

"Don't be so hard on yourself."

These are lies straight from the pit of hell. It is true that when we sin, we have an advocate with the Father. He is the Holy Spirit, the Paraclete. A paraclete is much like an attorney who goes before the judge and pleads our case. The Holy Spirit goes to the Father and says, "He or she has repented. They have asked for forgiveness and the Blood of Jesus has covered their sin. It is no more. It is your Son that you see." God looks from His throne and sees only radiance shinning from us. The Holy Spirit is the One who is always at our side. No matter what we do or where we go, no matter what we are going through, He is right there with us. As I write this, I am thrilled once again with the unmerited gift that Jesus gave us.

Do I understand that this Jesus of Nazareth, Son of the Most High God, Creator of the Universe, the Omnipotent One, in all His majesty, would give His life and shed His blood for me? Consider how much He loves you and me to have died for us! For just a moment think about that, think about the amount of love it takes to go through the beatings and humiliation Jesus Christ went through all the while knowing it would end in His death. If you were the only person in the world, He still would have loved you enough to die you.

No, I cannot begin to understand or even begin to comprehend it. But I do know that God is not a man that He should lie, and if He said it, I believe it. That by two immutable things, in which it was impossible for God to lie, we might have a strong consolation, who have fled for refuge to lay hold upon the hope set before us (Hebrews 6:18).

Summary and Reflection

God loves you and is lonesome for you!

Thou shalt not be afraid for the terror by night; nor for the arrow that flieth by day, Psalms 91:5. He never leaves you. He never fails you. He loves you!

My goodness, and my fortress; my high tower, and my deliverer; my shield, and he in whom I trust; who subdueth my people under me (Psalm 144:2). These are all ways He shows His love for us.

But now, O Lord, thou art our Father, we are the clay and thou our potter (Isaiah 64:8).

The fear of the Lord tendeth to life; and he that hath it shall abide satisfied; he shall not be visited with evil (Proverbs 19:23). You are protected by His love and mercy.

I will instruct thee and teach thee in the way which thou shalt go: I will guide thee with mine eye (Psalm 32:8). He is our teacher. He brings us to salvation and eternal life. Not because He has to, but because He loves us so much He wants us with Him always.

I am come that they might have life, and that they might have it more abundantly (John 10:10). His love gives us life and joy.

Chapter 17
Celebrate Others. They are also God's creation.

Have you ever worked or lived with someone who is just so caught up in themselves that you can't stand it? Maybe we are all that way at times. We all need times where we are the center of attention. We can forgive that in ourselves but don't like to see it in others. Often what annoys us about someone else is ourselves being reflected back. God created each person uniquely to be celebrated because no two people are the same. He created each person to be wholly individual, but still in His image. I am sure we can find fault in anyone, but to find a cause to celebrate is a testament to our belief and trust in God. People can't change without God's love evidenced in each of us.

Not too long ago, at my eldest daughter's birthday party, she and I were talking at length about something to do with her job. Suddenly, my youngest daughter spoke up and said, "Enough of that, let's talk about me."

She was joking and we all laughed, but there are people who seriously feel that way. They only want to hear about themselves and talk about themselves. They have a need to celebrate themselves constantly. They are the best at everything and will even put others down in order to get ahead. They have no concept of an eternal God who created every one of us wonderfully.

It is frustrating when others act that way. I just want to thump them and sometimes, to be honest, their attitudes can be very annoying. It's then that God reminds me of how inferior they truly feel. They do not know or understand His love. They do not realize how He specifically and uniquely created each of them exactly the way He wanted them to be. They are not aware of the mission our precious Father placed them here to accomplish. They seem to try and get in everyone else's mission and business because they're lost.

Many are running in circles; they believe if they speak loudly enough, put others down enough, it will make them look better and feel better. But they are a product and result of their upbringing and lives; whatever happened to cause them to appear almost narcissistic in their life has only served to cause them to appear and feel less than others. They are afraid.

There are millions of people scurrying around the earth attempting to find their purpose. Many do not know God loves them unconditionally. Either they have never been taught or have never settled long enough to hear His voice tell them of the great love He has for them. They do not know what direction to go.

My eldest daughter began college and thought she needed to study exactly what I had studied. I was a psychology major and she felt the best thing to do was excel in the same field. She dropped out of psychology after a year and said to me, "Mom, I could never take people telling me their problems all day. I would go crazy."

I was made by God to do that, but she always excelled in electronics and computers. We tried to tell her to study that field, but she continued to deny that was the field she was gifted in. We continued to pray as we observed her going from one job to another, never satisfied.

Eventually, she learned of a position working with computers through her younger sister. At first she was too afraid to apply but she did, and was hired. She is now a Web administrator and Web designer. She repairs all the computers at two country clubs and loves her job. She may gripe about long days and people who don't understand computers, but there is a satisfaction and peace in her that was a long time coming. This is the kind of joy that all of us can experience when we go in the direction our precious Father intended for us.

She is serving God by repairing computers because she is using the gift He put in her. She is at peace with herself. She can provide for herself and her son. She can tithe as God instructed her to do. She pays her bills. Most importantly, she is happy

I was too involved in getting my own messed up life right. She thought if she were just like me I would love her more. What a terrible picture of God's love I must have given her at that time. No excuses. I was divorced, raising three children, and still not knowing who God was. I was terrified. I was petrified I would fail my family, my children, myself, and my employers. I believed I was a total failure. Therefore, I became a harsh disciplinarian. It was all I knew. I wanted to make absolutely sure that my children never made the mistakes (sins) that I had. I was going to make sure they were better than I was. None of us can guarantee that, though. *For all have sinned, and come short of the glory of God, being justified freely by his grace through the redemption that is in Christ Jesus* (Romans 3:23-24). Every one of us has sinned and will sin. It is only through the grace and blood of Jesus Christ that we are made worthy. There are days when I feel the only thing I have accomplished is going to the Father at least a thousand times to ask forgiveness. On those days, I wonder if I will ever get it right. *Being justified freely by His grace through the redemption that is in Christ Jesus: Whom God hath set forth to be a propitiation though faith in His blood, to declare His righteousness for the remission of sins that are past, through the forbearance of God* (Romans 3:24-25).

Because of God's graciousness, both of my daughters and my son have forgiven me the mistakes of my past; we've talked about it many times and have become true friends, in addition to the gift of being mother and child. Today, we can laugh together as no one else can. I can hardly breathe. But it is good healing laughter. Who are the friends that you have who are able to make you laugh like this? They are the ones that who celebrate you.

The absolute first step in becoming celebrated is the step from your feet to your knees. Get on your knees before an omnipotent Creator and ask for the gift of Jesus Christ into your heart. Ask forgiveness for your sins and come to the realization that without Christ you are nothing. Ask Him to guide your life and be open to His leading. Trusting in Him in all matters is to become celebrated.

It takes only a few minutes for the action but a lifetime of listening and obedience to fulfill.

It is a lifetime of peace and true joy.

It is a lifetime of feeling equal to anyone we meet, whether it be kings or presidents. We are all equal in God's eyes.

For there is no difference between the Jew and the Greek: for the same Lord over all is rich unto all that call upon Him (Romans 10:12).

There is neither Jew nor Greek, there is neither bond nor free, there is neither male nor female: for ye are all one in Christ Jesus (Galatians 3:28).

I wonder how many of you believe that your life has a mission? Not just on Sunday or at home with your family, but everywhere you are, including your workplace.

Many of you may believe that I'm completely off-base here. In the first place, we have laws that ensure we do not and cannot witness in our places of work. Hmmm! I do not believe that is how God planned it or sees it. He wants us to witness every place our little bodies go, including work. I do not mean that you trot off to work and proceed to preach a sermon or enter work and gaze at the person who gives you the most difficulty and say, "Repent!" That may get you fired—or at the least, analyzed.

However, it is through relationships that we see ourselves. They mirror back to us just who we are. It is also through those relationships that our mission is carried out.

Perhaps God placed us in that position to pray for just one person (quietly). Perhaps He placed us there to show others, especially non-believers, exactly what a Christian (Christ like) is supposed to be. Are we a good example? Or do we gossip at lunch and play with our computers at our desks?

Do we let others pick up our slack?

Do we preach to everyone about how they should become Christians and become as "perfect" as we are?

Do we laugh at dirty jokes, or worse, tell them?

Do we always come to work with a miserable scowl on our faces and wonder why co-workers attempt to avoid us?

Do we tell our bosses how important we are to them and the company without any evidence to back it up?

Who would want to become a Christian and share in our misery?

Do we realize that our workplaces are places of trust in which God has positioned us? That a loving God would consider us worthy to be situated into a particular place to show His loving kindness, His ethics, His order, is completely beyond me. Do we, do I, show myself worthy? No, we don't, and neither do I. I have fallen short. There are times that I am a whiny baby, exactly like many others in the world. I want my way and I want it now! I want to be recognized. I want my work to be easier.

. . .*And the labourer is worthy of his reward* (2 Timothy 5:18b). Our reward is the wages we are paid for our employment, but our real gift is the approval, love, and trust that our Father has given us and will give us when we finally are with Him in heaven. What a glorious homecoming when He says, "Welcome, My good and faithful servant."

His lord said unto him, Well done,
thou good and faithful servant: thou hast
been faithful over a few things, I will make
thee ruler over many things; enter thou into
the joy of thy lord (Matthew 25:21).

What a blessed time that will be! All of His promises will be given to us for a few moments of obedience and service here on earth. What a reward!

I know that we cannot fly through life like Mary Poppins, with our magical umbrella taking us from one happy place to another. Each of us has struggles and trials that we must endure and triumph over. It is the humbling of ourselves, prostrate before the Lord of the universe, and telling Him that we are nothing without Him that gets us through those struggles and trials.

If there are fellow Christians in your neighborhood, you need to seek them out. If there are non-Christians in your neighborhood, you need to seek them and love them into the body of Christ. Sometimes the best friends you will ever make are the ones you never thought would be. Remember when you were a child, how many of the children you fought with became your best friends? The loyal friends of Jesus stood by Him unto the end and beyond. They were the ones willing to lay down their lives for Him. Looking at the apostles and disciples from the outside, you would not have thought they would be the ones to stand beside Jesus no matter what. They accepted His friendship and loved Him in faith, they were closer than brothers. The prostitute at the well became the friend of Jesus. How many of us would look to a prostitute to become our friend? We often look at outward appearances without seeing the intentions of God within the person. Outward actions in others can often be the result of hurts suffered from another. How many people have you excused from a possible friendship because of outward appearance? Often the actions of others are hiding a lifetime of hurt. Sometimes we have to love and celebrate that child of God to the surface. That person may become your best friend. We need to look at others as Jesus saw us and as He sees them. Celebrate the unique.

Summary and Reflection

A man that hath friends must shew himself friendly: and there is a friend that sticketh closer than a brother (Proverbs 18:24).

A friend loveth at all times (Proverbs 17:17a).

Go out and celebrate at least one person that you might not have thought would be or could be a friend.

Chapter 18
Growing Up into Christ and in the Body

For many years I attended a particular Christian church in Oregon, and continue to attend that denomination where I now live. I have visited many churches inside and outside of my denomination and have also found welcome love, acceptance, and Jesus Christ in them.

My church in Oregon was the first time I went to church and found the pastor wearing jeans. Often during the summer he would wear Bermuda shorts and we would have services out on the hillside, as Jesus did. He read the gospels, chapter and verse from Genesis to Revelations. I learned so much in that body of believers. What we wore made no difference. Who we were made no difference. They loved and welcomed everyone. While I was ministering on the streets, I brought many who were homeless with me. They didn't have clean clothing, but they were loved and fed. I have since witnessed this in so many churches across our country.

The Church is where we go for fellowship and comfort. We attend to grow in the Lord and to honor Him. We need that close relationship in our church that we find nowhere else. We need that connection with our brothers and sisters. We also need the tender discipline and direction that we receive from our pastors.

We need to support our churches in spirit, in love, and financially. I don't mean just the building but everyone in it, whether members or not. The Church is the complete body of Christ and not just a building. It is for everyone who believes or wants to find Him.

God asked us to tithe, and once we obey the Lord, trust your church to do what is right. Tithing is an important discipline that our Lord taught us. Jesus said that as we give we receive, but that is not the reason for tithing. The reason is that God has given us everything and asks for but a small portion to be returned through the Church and missions.

Have you ever had a time where there was nowhere else to turn but to your pastor and the body of believers? They are your supporters. They are our example of Christ on earth. Jesus and the disciples ministered to everyone they encountered. They forgave. They healed. They blessed the people. That's what we receive from our body of believers. In turn, we must give back to the body. We must love them, care for them, and support them in every way. There are people who need help and have nowhere to turn but the Church. Many need food, shelter, medical care. The Church has many needs and cannot fulfill them unless we support the Church.

Do you have a gift that you can share with your church? Are you a medical person of some type? Are you a builder? Are you a counselor? What about being a farmer? Can you cook for the needy? Can you help a disabled or elderly person clean their home or get to an appointment? Is someone in your church looking for employment and you are in need of an employee? There are so many ways in addition to tithing where we need to be responsible in our churches and communities.

I'm sure you've recognized that there are times when the only person you can talk to about problems is your pastor or an elder in your church. We also need to help with the burden the pastor and elders often have. Can we listen to a brother or sister whose heart is hurting because of a problem in their lives? As much as the body of believers needs us, we need them even more. They are our comfort and strength here on earth.

Growing up in Christ and in our Body of Believers is central to the Christian life. They are the ones who will keep us on track. They will celebrate us and counsel us.

Summary and Reflection

The meek will He guide in judgment: and the meek will he teach his way (Psalms 25:9).

He that followeth Me shall not walk in darkness (John 8:12b).

It is not in man that walketh to direct his steps (Jeremiah 10:23).

I will instruct thee in the way which thou shalt go: I will guide thee with mine eye (Psalms 32:8).

That we henceforth be no more children, tossed to and fro, and carried about with every wind of doctrine, by the sleight of men, and cunning craftiness, whereby they lie in wait to deceive (Ephesians 4:14).

Be not forgetful to entertain strangers: for thereby some have entertained angels unaware. Remember them that are in bonds, as bound with them; and them which suffer adversity, as being yourselves also in the body (Hebrews 13:1-3).

Chapter 19
Bringing God Pleasure

Have you ever thought that you bring God pleasure?

Of course, you do. Each of us does when we accept Jesus as our Savior. The host of Heaven rejoices at one lost sinner returning to the fold. That same host of Heaven rejoices when they see us walking in the way of the Lord and walking as though Christ truly lived within us.

Many mornings when I drove to my office, it was still dark, but I could see a beautiful white hybrid wolf standing in the country road. I always slowed or slightly swerved to avoid it. It was tall, muscular, and stately in its presence. I wondered, "What if God has sent an angel in this form?"

One afternoon as I was driving home, I saw it dead and lying on the road. I cried for that animal. It was a magnificent creation of God.

Have you ever danced before the Lord? What a joyous and freeing experience that is. I love the song "And David Danced."

I'm sure that King David did indeed dance. The Bible said he danced with all his might. Imagine what that must have looked like. The Lord had seen fit to forgive his sins and David felt the joy of that reprieve.

But God has also seen fit to forgive our sins, and I'm sure that when we dance or sing before the Lord in joy, all of heaven smiles. I'll never get over the gift that God has given us in Jesus Christ. King David looked forward to the coming of Jesus Christ, the Messiah. He had no human guarantee that the Messiah would come. He stood in faith and believed it would happen one day. He had heard the stories and knew what God said would come about.

He waited with expectation and not doubt. We have His coming to look back at, as hope of His return. The prophecy has been fulfilled. It should be so much easier for us to believe and accept His wonderful gift.

The saints of the Old Testament had only the promise of what would come. They also sinned, but in my thinking, it seems more forgivable for them. They were awaiting the coming. They lived by faith.

We are awaiting His second coming. We live by faith, too.

If He came the first time, He will return. Even Mary, the mother of Jesus, must have doubted after the angel came to tell her that she would be the mother of the Messiah. That really would have been a challenge for me to tell anyone if I had been Mary. I would wonder, "Are they going to think I've gone crazy and have me committed?" And I could just see me telling my husband—who, by the way, is a really good man, but I think even he could believe just so much.

I can just imagine it....

"Sanford, I need to tell you that I'm pregnant, but you aren't the father." That would have started things on a downward spiral.

Then I would have told him, "But Honey, God is the Father. It was a miracle of God."

Would he have thought I was totally crazy? Thankfully, God went to Mary and not to any of us. I would have asked God if He minded putting it on the national news and in all the leading newspapers. Then, I would have asked Him if He minded going directly to Sanford, my husband, and setting him straight.

Mary trusted. Can you imagine the faith all of that would have taken? I never think too much of Joseph, but he must have lived a faithful life to the Lord to have accepted all of it. Even when he had the dream telling him about it, he might have sworn it was something he had eaten. I probably would never have believed it. That is the faith we all need to get a grip on and not let go.

When God sends us a word or a sign, He wants us to believe and not doubt Him. We must remember that what He asks of us or directs us to do will always align with His word.

Do you ever do something nice for no reason at all and for no credit? That's the Holy Spirit working through you, and that always brings God pleasure.

Do you ever wake up in the morning and begin praising God for another day of life, another day to serve Him? That's the Holy Spirit in you, and that always brings God pleasure.

Do you ever do a job really well, to the best of your ability, at work or at home and not try to take extra credit? That's the Holy Spirit, and that always brings God pleasure.

Do you ever just quietly pick up your Bible and begin reading, as unto the Lord? That, too, is the Holy Spirit, and that always brings God pleasure.

What about praying for those you don't even know, all across the world? The Word says to pray even for those who despitefully use you (Luke 6:28).

The Word says that we do not even know how to pray, and that we should ask the Holy Spirit to pray through us.

Believing Him and trusting Him always brings God pleasure.

All of those things bring smiles to the heavens.

We are God's kids. He loves us. He wants to be proud of us. Somehow, I can just imagine God nudging Elijah or one of the prophets of old, and saying, "Look! That's my child there!"

God cannot wait for the day that we return to Him in heaven. He longs for us to be there with Him. That is the sole reason we were created. He wants to enjoy us. But even more than that, He wants us to enjoy Him! Oh, yes! What a wonderful, miraculous event that will be!

I have read the description of heaven so many times in the book of Revelation and yet, I think, none of its beauty will matter. We will stand in the presence of the Father, the Son, and the Holy Spirit. We will commune with them. All of the questions that we have had all of our lives will matter no longer. All of the hurts, the pains, the sorrows that we have had will be gone, never remembered.

I think of those who have been martyred for the sake of the Lord, those who have suffered throughout their lives, those who have been beaten, tortured, killed, molested even unto the point of death, those who have frozen to death on our rich nation's sidewalks and alleyways, and I think. I think, "Surely Lord, they will sit a little closer to You." Then, I remember that it will all be gone. The only things remembered will be the Lord of Hosts and the joys of heaven.

God is so much smarter than any of us.

He has always picked the ordinary and fallible sinners like you and me to reach others with His message of salvation. I do not remember any high-ranking persons that God usually uses for His purposes.

Even Albert Einstein, one of my favorite people, said, "Let me know God's thoughts, the rest are details."

He was even speaking of himself. He knew he wasn't important in the great scheme of things. But God will always use what we are willing to give Him.

Long ago, I never thought I would speak publicly. I would stutter and perspire profusely when I was called on, even in a classroom. I also remember as an undergraduate, telling God that I would speak for Him if He should ever think that was necessary. I told Him that the Holy Spirit would have to speak through me, though, because no one would ever want to hear anything I had to say.

Would you like to know where has God placed me? I speak in front of large groups all of the time. Has God ever done that for you? He showed you that through Him you are already equipped to do anything. I've had to appear on newscasts several times to speak about my church or my profession. Do I continue to stutter and perspire? Not unless it's really warm.

God has used my insecurities to help others that He would have me reach. I remember an author saying that when we give up what we're holding away from God, then God can take our hand and hold us up. What a thrilling thing to go through. God doesn't want scholars—not that He can't use them; He just wants us, ordinary, fallible humans that He created.

We bring Him pleasure. We do. Wow…

Summary and Reflection

Have you ever stood in front of your mirror in the morning and wondered, "How can I bring my God pleasure today?"

Be ye therefore followers of God, as dear children; and walk in love, as Christ also hath loved us, and hath given himself for us an offering and a sacrifice to God for a sweetsmelling savour (Ephesians 5:1-2).

Read the entire chapter of Ephesians 5 and meditate on it. It gives us clear direction on how to please Him. If there is some way that we want to bring God pleasure, check your scripture to make sure it lines up with what He has already told us. If we feel the least doubt, reexamine it and go back to Him, asking for direction.

We are not here to serve self-pleasing men or women. We are here to please our God and no one else. Of course, in pleasing Him, we will always place others before ourselves. Remember how Mother Teresa gave of herself, to her dying breath? We may not all be called to live as she did, but we are all called to love others and minister to them.

He hath shewed thee, O man, what is good; and what doth the Lord require of thee, but to do justly, and to love mercy, and to walk humbly with thy God? (Micah 6:8).

Chapter 20
We All Have a Place in the Plan

I am passionate about helping others and have been this way ever since I can remember. As a child, I just knew that I wanted to grow up and help people who were hurting.

My husband has a need to lead and encourage others. My oldest daughter is a fixer. She will fix anything, sometimes even people. My son is an encourager and an uplifter. He always has the right thing to say to make you feel better. My youngest daughter is an organizer and a motivator. She wants to motivate the world for the Lord.

I'm not sure if they all even know what they're doing, but I observe each of them working in a different way but for the same ultimate purpose. They lead others to do their best for their own lives, for the good of others, and to the glory of God.

Each of us is different in the calling God has placed in our lives. We may look up to another and think that we would really like to do what the other person is doing, but unless God has called us and placed that particular gift and passion in us, we will grow weary in it. He knew us from our mother's womb. God places the call or vocation in our life but will only give us what He knows we can do.

I have not been called to pastor a church. If I did it on my own, without God's calling, I would make a disaster of it. But I am called to help others; God, in His wisdom, has placed me in HIV/AIDS prevention, education, and testing. I have also been called to counsel those with mental health problems.

I could say that I wound up here by accident, but there are no accidents in the life of a Christian. I am exactly where I am supposed to be at this time in my life and doing exactly what I'm supposed to be doing.

God has graciously given me the opportunity to witness to so many people that I would never have had the occasion to meet if I were doing anything else. I also can pray for those I come in contact with, whether they turn out HIV-positive or negative. Isn't it incredible that God took me all the way from Oregon to Oklahoma to North Carolina to work for Him?

Look at where you are. No matter what you're going through, God has positioned you right now. Even if it seems like you're off course or spinning your wheels, God has you there to make a divine connection that will advance your purpose here on earth.

God is the One for whom I ultimately work. God is the One for whom you ultimately work, too. My agency may have hired me, but it was God who inspired that hiring. This does not mean it is where I will always be. God may have a different plan for my life in the next day or two. If He does, I will be willing to go where He calls.

Are you working somewhere right now and wondering why you are there? If you are, then search the heart of God for the reason you're there. It may be to witness to just one person whom God has been trying to reach. It may not be the place where you will always be, but you certainly belong there right now.

Again, there are no mistakes made by God. It is our job to find out where we belong and why. None of us pretend to know the mind of God, but God may have placed you there for one person. I do know that when God's time is right, we will be placed wherever else He wants for His ultimate purpose.

Are we ever positive that we are where God wants us? I don't think so, but if we are in the wrong place, God will move us. Wherever we are, He will fill a need for His purposes. We must be open to His leading.

I recently endured two separate surgeries within a two-month period. I took off one day for the first surgery and with the second surgery, I had the weekend to recuperate a bit. I found myself tired and worn. I work in a five-county area and am constantly busy. Some days I work late into the evenings. I have always been an early riser and prefer to go to bed early. I was tired, and I began feeling sorry for myself.

Do you ever feel like that? You start to think about the things you'd rather be doing instead of focusing on what you ARE doing. I wondered if I should quit work and just stay home with my husband. I enjoy my home looking nice and I used to enjoy cooking. I also enjoy my time with my husband. He's quiet but enjoyable and supportive. I thought I could easily do that again. I know many women who stay home and their homes are always spotless. They usually have a nice warm meal on the table at dinnertime, too. My husband endures many evenings of salads, sandwiches, and hot dogs. Praise God he isn't a complainer, though.

As I thought about this, I began praying about it. I figured when all else fails, I better follow directions. I wanted God's will, not mine, even though mine sounded pretty good to me. I waited and waited, and suddenly I realized I didn't mind working anymore. I was okay. I also realized that God had placed three people in my life, through my work, that I would not have been able to witness to if I was not working. My thinking changed from thoughts of quiet comfort at home to thoughts of how much God must love those three people to want them so badly. They don't even know Him yet, but I believe they will. It may take quite a while, but if God could be so patient with me, I'll be patient with them and with my own life.

One of those three people believes that God is in every faith, religion, tree, desk, etc. One believes that God is a great energy field that each of us can tap into and become like gods. The Bible clearly states that there is only one true God. In Exodus, God gave us the commandment "Do not worship any other gods besides me" (Exodus 20:3).

We can and often do make anything and everything into a god. We want control and we want to be in command of our lives. If we can convince ourselves that God is something or someone that we can just tap into and become as gods ourselves, and then we hold the reins. We think we are god. We set these gods up so that we do not have to assume accountability to anyone outside of ourselves. What we decide is right becomes so, at least to our own thinking.

No one else dare tell us we are wrong. We just have to tell them how narrow they are in their thinking.

Of course, anything can be justified by doing that. Hitler felt justified in killing 6 million Jews. Horrible atrocities have been done in the name of God. People have been tortured and killed because of their belief or because of their skin color.

This is not the true God. It is not the God that I serve.

Our God is the God of Abraham and Moses. The same God who told the children of Israel, after leaving Egypt, to "take" the land of Canaan! He is the God who created all things and gave us the commandments. It is He who rescued us from slavery, He who gave free will to humankind and even gave us the choice to sin. It is He who lived, died, and was resurrected. It is He who will return in the clouds for all to see. Every knee will bow at His return. Only He is infallible! He is our God!

And this Great and Mighty God takes the time to place each of us exactly where we will be most fulfilled and where we will walk in our call. We all have a place in The Plan.

Summary and Reflection

Read 1 Corinthians Chapter 12, 13, and 14

And He gave some, apostles; and some, prophets; and some evangelists; and some, pastors and teachers; for the perfecting of the saints, for the work of the ministry, for the edifying of the body of Christ: Till we all come in the unity of the faith, and of the knowledge of the Son of god unto a perfect man, unto the measure of the stature of the fullness of Christ (Ephesians 4:11-13).

Do you know what your gift is? Have you prayed about your gift? Have you asked for confirmation? Every person in the Body has a gift; ask God today what your gift is. Don't rush, wait for His answer! Think about the things you love doing at church and for others. Your gift may be there. Search for God's plan in your life.

Neglect not the gift that is in thee, which was given thee by prophecy, with the laying on of the hands of the presbytery. Meditate upon these things; give thyself wholly to them; that thy profiting may appear to all. Take heed unto thyself, and unto the doctrine; continue in them: for in doing this thou shalt both save thyself, and them that hear thee (1 Timothy 4:14-16).

Now concerning spiritual gifts, brethren, I would not have you ignorant. Ye know that ye were Gentiles, carried away unto these dumb idols, even as ye were led. Wherefore I give you to understand that no man speaking by the Spirit of God calleth Jesus accursed: and that no man can say that Jesus is the Lord, but by the Holy Ghost. Now there are diversities of gifts, but the same Spirit. And there are differences of administrations, but the same Lord. And there are diversities of operations, but it is the same God which worketh all in all. But the manifestation of the Spirit is given to every man to profit withal. For to one is given by the Spirit the word of wisdom; to another the word of knowledge by the same Spirit; To another faith by the same Spirit; to another the gifts of healing by the same Spirit; To another the working of miracles; to another prophecy; to another divers kinds of tongues; to another the interpretation of tongues: But all these worketh that one and the selfsame Spirit, dividing to every man severally as he will. For as the body is one, and hath many members, and all the members of that one body, being many, are one body: so also is Christ. For by one Spirit are we all baptized into one body, whether we be Jews or Gentiles, whether we be bond or free; and have been all made to drink into one Spirit (1 Corinthians 12:1-13).

Carefully study each of the gifts. Where do you see yourself fitting in? Which gift do you think you have? Are you using your gift? Praise God and begin using the gift He has given you. In His divine plan each of us already has a gift. Celebrate yours!

But speak thou the things which become sound doctrine: that the aged men be sober, grave, temperate, sound in faith, in charity, in patience. The aged women likewise, that they be in behavior as becometh holiness, not false accusers, not given to much wine, teachers of good things; that they may teach the young women to be sober, to love their husbands, to love their children, to be discreet, chaste, keepers at home, good, obedient to their own husbands, that the world of God be not blasphemed. Young men likewise exhort to be sober minded. In all things shewing thyself a pattern of good work: in doctrine shewing uncorruptness, gravity, sincerity, sound speech, that cannot be condemned; that he that is of the contrary part may be having, having no evil thing to say of you (Titus 2:1-8).

These words are excellent examples for how to live our lives according to God's plan.

Chapter 21
My Lord

I have been getting myself in a dither lately noticing that I just do not hear Christians proclaiming Jesus Christ as Lord and Savior. I believe others are getting tired of hearing me ask if Jesus Christ is indeed their Lord and Savior and if He is, let me hear it.

Why aren't we professing it?

None of us can be a Christian without accepting the lordship of Jesus Christ. He is the one and only way we have to Father God. It is imperative that every single person claiming to be a Christian profess Him the Lord. *That if thou shalt confess with thy mouth the Lord Jesus, and shalt believe in thin heart that God hath raised him from the dead, thou shalt be saved* (Romans 10:9).

What is the problem?

Have we become so sophisticated that it is no longer necessary?

I love the Lord with all of my soul and being. Why? I was a sinner. I still am, but now know that if I ask forgiveness, He is faithful and just to give it. I was living a life of sin that never brought me happiness. I hated myself and hated everyone. I often thought of and even attempted suicide several times. I thought a life of drinking, sex, drugs, and a fast life would help me to love myself. It never did until one day the Lord Himself told me He loved me. He wanted "nothing" of me but my allegiance to Him.

Only Jesus Christ is to have the power, authority, and ownership of our lives. He is our divine ruler. 1 Corinthians 8:6 says: *But to us there is but one God, the Father, of whom are all things, and we in him; and one Lord Jesus Christ, by whom are all things, and we by him.*

Jesus is the reason for our existence. He is our Master and Ruler. He is also our personal Savior. He is also the world's Savior. He is our healer. But unless we believe as Romans tells us that He is the Lord and Master of our lives, then He is not Lord and Master. Who is in control if He is not; are we? Is the world? Are new-age ideas flooding over us and causing us to be ashamed of His majesty? Are we a fast-food type of religion?

The new Christian, and many old ones, don't realize that they must proclaim that Lordship of Christ. Our new spirit man/woman, when we become saved, doesn't know that we live by faith, no longer by the flesh.

New Christians need to be taught to give their flesh to the Lordship of Christ. We fight it. We've lived so long in these fleshly bodies that we don't have any clue how to act spiritually and stand in the faith we've recently accepted. We look for acceptance and love in the world, and we fail to look to the most perfect love that we may ever experience. We (women) look for a man who will fulfill all of our needs and become our hero. He will always be there to take care of us and save us from the scary things of the world.

Men look for a woman who will take care of them and be a credit to them in the world's eyes. She will be the woman all other men desire. We "think" we have it so together when we believe that we've found that someone. We've made it! Or so we would believe. . .

But unless our first love is the Lord, all else will fail us. It's not even the other person's fault. It's that we're looking for that pure and perfect love that is found in no one other than Jesus Christ, the pure and perfect Lamb of God, who was tortured, spit on, whipped, beaten, ridiculed, and killed in the most inhumane manner, for you, for me, and for each one of us. That is the pure and perfect love that we are seeking. He is the only One who can fulfill the desires of our hearts and souls.

We need to learn to get "on fire" for the Lord. Getting on fire is not sitting at home reading scripture and watching television evangelists, unless you are too ill to leave your home. It's not sitting in a church pew spouting how proud we are—in a humble manner, of course—of the minor acts or thoughts we have.

It's truly getting on fire. It's living solely for the Lord! It's praying without ceasing! It's caring for the person sitting next to you at church or across the aisle. Caring enough that you get motivated to act rather than asking everyone to pray for that person who has a need.

Saying "Good morning" and "God bless you" doesn't count, either. What about meeting the real needs of another person? Does an elder person in the church need someone to visit and help clean or someone to prepare and deliver a meal? Do they need a dress or a pair of slacks pressed? Has someone's telephone been turned off because of a lack of funds? If you cannot pay it yourself, in secret, can you get several to come together quietly and meet the payment? What about their electric bill or heating bill? Those things are necessary wherever you live.

The Word says not to let your right hand know what your left is doing. The Word also says that when we do an act of kindness, we shouldn't do it as the Pharisees did, by letting everyone know.

Is someone in need of food to put on the family table?

Is someone lonely or heartbroken? Can you spend the time going to them and listening? Can you offer comfort?

Are there those in your church who have no family? No one to visit them or to go and visit? What about a simple hug, a heartfelt hug?

Does a single mother or father have the need for someone to help mentor her or his child? Could someone use help doing a load of laundry or ironing (yes, some still iron)?

Is there a single man or husband with a handicapped wife, who could use some cooking lessons?

Is there a rowdy teen that needs acceptance and perhaps help with homework?

Are there people on the streets who could use a warm jacket or a hot meal? Don't worry if they are Christians. Many are Christians who feel no other Christian really cares for them. Do as Jesus did. Feed the hungry, shelter the homeless, heal the brokenhearted. That is praying without ceasing! That is permitting the Lord to live within you. That's also the way to witness to others and bring them to the Lord. Let your actions be your prayers and praise.

When I first accepted the Lord and joined the Christian family I thought I was such a "good" Christian. I had stopped using drugs and drinking alcohol. I stopped going out dancing and all the nonsense that accompanied it. I was good! I had it together! I even felt a little self-righteous. I was also observing other Christians and certainly didn't see them doing all that I was. I had a wonderful testimony. Of course, the problem was that it was my testimony of myself, not the testimony of the Lord. I was taking credit for everything, even my own salvation. "I" got saved! I didn't even give the Lord full credit for that.

Of course, the Lord had to knock me to my knees. That's where I should have been all along, on my knees. I should have been crying out to Him and weeping for the unsaved, in my prayer closet. (A prayer closet is nothing more than a place, a room, wherever, that enables you to be quiet and undisturbed. It can even be your automobile.) I should have been seeking His guidance instead of my own.

I no longer see myself as better than the world. The Lord has shown me that I am a hopeless mess without Him.

I've found that I'm not so angry with others anymore. It's none of my business what they're doing for the Lord. The Lord calls us all differently according to His will. I openly tell others now that I'm not even worthy to be God's worst. I'm just a sinner saved by the grace of God.

Others look at me when I tell them what a sinner I am. I've been told to remember that Jesus forgives me sins and that I should not keep saying that I am a sinner. But I am a sinner only saved by His grace. What good would it do to not say it? We are all sinners. I wonder what would happen if the entire church body became transparent? Would we all be aghast at our neighbor's and fellow church member's sins? Would we be shocked to find our ministers are sinful? Or would we go to them in love and ask how we might help, all the while being fully aware that we also are sinners?

What if I truly shared my deepest needs with the church? Would anyone come to help me or would they shun me, afraid of my openness? It makes us uncomfortable when we realize someone we love or care for is no better or worse than any unsaved person. We don't like to see the uglies.

People say I'm too hard on myself at times. Perhaps I am, but the one thing each of us needs to realize is that we have a desperate need for Jesus in our lives. That's what we have in common. We are all sinners, saved by the Blood of the Lamb. We are not the Savior, but we sure are in need of Him. We need a Savior because we are sinners, and the wages of sin is death.

Before I was afflicted, I went astray; but now I keep thy word. Thou art good and doest good; teach me thy statutes. I know, O Lord, that thy judgments are right, and that in faithfulness thou hast afflicted me. Let thy steadfast love be ready to comfort me according to thy promise to thy servant (Psalm 119:67, 68, 71, 75, 76).

Behold, I have refined thee, but not with silver; I have chosen thee in the furnace of affliction (Isaiah 48:10).

Jesus Christ is the only one to have the authority, power, ownership, and rule in our lives.

Ye call me Master and Lord: and ye say well; for so I am" (John 13:13).

Summary and Reflection

But when they shall lead you, and deliver you up, take no thought beforehand what ye shall speak, neither do ye premeditate: but whatsoever shall be given you in that hour, that speak ye: for it is not ye that speak, but the Holy Ghost (Mark 13:11).

For the Holy Ghost shall teach you in the same hour what ye ought to say (Luke 12:12).

Reflect on who the Lord Jesus Christ really is to you. Reflect and remember that His coming was foretold thousands of years before He ever appeared as an infant. Reflect on how much He really loves you. Meditate on your sins being washed clean. Think about having an entirely new life, where sin has never entered. It makes no difference what you have done; He is there to cover you with His Blood. No more condemnation! He took the condemnation from you, and by His stripes you are healed.

Accept that you are a miracle because of Him and His willingness and obedience to the Father. Accept that the Father loved you before you were ever thought of. Accept that no matter where you go or what you do, the Holy Spirit is right there with you. When you look in the mirror and condemn yourself for another failure, know that the Holy Spirit stands with you. Know that no matter what path you take, the Holy Spirit walks with you, beside you, and leads you.

Chapter 22
True Shepherds

Have you ever attended a church and lived fearful of the pastor and the rest of the flock? Have you ever been afraid of the judgment that would come upon you if you ever admitted to the body that you were a sinner or admitted a particular fault or sin?

Have you ever just wanted to run away from the Church? I have! I'm talking about the ones who are so filled with themselves and their abilities that they do not have time for the Holy Spirit to really take hold. He didn't ordain those types! They are self-appointed pastors and they're usually in their position for the money or the prestige. The need for prestige and adulation are strong motivators for many. It is a motivator that can lead someone straight to hell. Pastors today are getting caught in sexual immorality, drugs, thievery, and every sin imaginable. We, as the Church, need to keep our pastors lifted up to the Lord and accountable for their actions. If we see them in sin, we need to be brave enough to confront them. If you saw a speeding truck coming at your pastor and he or she was not aware of it, wouldn't you scream, yell, push, shove, and do everything in your power to save him? This is more serious. This is their salvation.

I attended a certain church where the pastor would embarrass members into performing chores around the church and for him personally. I was terrified of him and felt that I would never be good enough. I don't mean that he would actually threaten me, but he would wait until a quiet time during the service and call on a member of the congregation. He would then instruct the church to lay hands on us and pray for deliverance. He used to enjoy doing that with my oldest daughter because he knew she would be embarrassed. She was always self-conscious, and I believe he could read people well. He attempted to embarrass and manipulate my daughter. I will always be sorry that I did not openly rebuke him the one time I witnessed it. My daughter is self-conscious, but she has always been headstrong as well. She finally said she was not going back and didn't.

One evening during worship service, we were all praying with our heads bowed and our eyes closed. I felt a tugging at my heart to look up. I tried to keep my head down but the tugging continued. Finally, I was obedient to the Lord and looked up at the pastor.

It wasn't the kindly appearing pastor I saw, but a demon from hell. His hair was disheveled and his nails were claws. His face was grotesque. The image so terrified me that I immediately walked out of the sanctuary; I could not go back. Two of my friends came after me and asked what was wrong. I shared my vision with them, and one said she felt a witness in her spirit when I told her. The other rebuked me and re-entered the sanctuary.

I could not attend the church after the vision, but the pastor began visiting my home unexpectedly. At first, he and his wife came alone, asking me to come back. I told him I could not come back. I told him I did not believe the Lord wanted me there. Then he began coming with church members and they would rebuke me and tell me that I was not acting in the Lord but out of my sinful nature. They wanted to lay hands on me and pray. I felt sure the Lord was telling me to not permit them to touch me or anyone in my family.

One night when we were all in bed asleep, the pastor came with his wife and sick child. Another couple from the church brought them. He begged me to permit him to use my new Jeep Cherokee to take his son to the hospital. I felt so bad for the child that I gave him permission and handed my keys over to him. He did not return my vehicle. I called the church, and he would hang up on me. I definitely had a leading from the Lord to stay away from the church.

A few days later, as I was praying, I felt the Lord telling me to call the FBI and ask about this pastor. After praying for a longer time, I couldn't shake the knowledge that God wanted me to call. I called the FBI and was told that this pastor was wanted in three or four states for bilking members out of their property and money. What I didn't know was that he had already had two members sell their homes and turn the money over to him. He told them they were leaving to minister around the country and that he would take complete care of them.

He and the members left before the FBI visited. About two years later, in a department store, I saw one of the elder women, a widow, who had gone with him, She told me that he didn't feed them or anything. She said they were all sleeping in one room together, on the floor. She thought he had left for Texas with his wife and children. About four years later, I heard that his youngest son was killed in an airplane crash. His other son had cerebral palsy.

Strive for the prize that is before us and give yesterday, or the last moment, to the Lord, knowing that when we confess to Him, forgiveness comes, the list of wrongs is deleted. It is made a blank page each time. What a gift he gives!

Do not ever let another person, pastor or not, belittle you, embarrass you, tell you that you are not worthy. Leave. Run, if you must, away from those. The Word says that all are not called by the Lord. Some come to deceive. How like the devil to find those who so desperately want to be committed to the Lord, but are damaged emotionally for some reason. He sneaks in, like a thief in the night, and sends one of his evil agents to work through another child to attempt to destroy the one who wants commitment.

Prideful Shepherds

I currently know a pastor of a local church who can never admit that he is wrong, has erred, or has even sinned. He must always appear as though he is without fault. He also cannot seem to forgive hurts of the past. I observe him occasionally and wonder when God will bring him on his knees to the foot of the Cross. When will he say, "It is finished because of you, Lord Jesus. I forgive as you forgave." I pray for him continually and even though I have not seen a result of my prayers, I know that "if" he is truly called by the Lord, he will truly become humble. This pastor is also caught up in sexual depravity and other sins, which could be what is blocking him from forgiveness for others.

Often we think because we're in a certain position, we are more knowledgeable than the "common" members of the Church. I need to repeat what I said earlier, we must hold our pastors and elders accountable for their actions.

By the same token, we must pay attention to our own lives. While pastors are held to a higher standard, we all are shepherding a flock of some kind. We influence the thoughts and actions of others by our own thoughts and actions. We must always be diligent in paying attention to what we are doing, if we are forgiving, where we are putting our attention, and how we are demonstrating Jesus.

Over my life, I have spoken to many who have walked away from the Church because of a hurt caused by a pastor or church member. I tell them, "But it's not the Lord who hurt you. He would never do that." Unfortunately, many people don't want to hear it. The hurt has been too deep and only confirmed what they previously believed. My heart aches for the hurt we do to each other. I have always heard that Christians are the only ones who kill their wounded. What a statement, but sadly, it's often true.

Getting Free

If the church you are currently attending does not teach a loving, forgiving Christ, get away from it. The Word says to "try the spirits to see if they are from God." Because you attend a certain church does not mean you can never leave that church. God may be directing you elsewhere. God cares about you and wants the Church to be a safe place, with a good shepherd tending the flock. If your shepherd does not tend to the members, find one who does. If he or she is not humble; not quick to forgive; is involved in sexual or other sin; or is prideful, run from the church as fast as your feet will carry you. If you stay, the shepherd may find a way to place blame on you instead of him/herself.

Often God will direct us to a different church for another reason. There may be nothing wrong with the church you are attending, but perhaps you are meant to be elsewhere to fulfill your ministry or to minister to another hurting soul.

I have also met many pastors who are on bended knee before the Lord continually. They are the ones praying for their congregation, for areas, for the world. They are also the ones planning and committing to the mission field. They are out there feeding the hungry, clothing the naked, giving of their humble resources to the poor and needy. They are the ones who have your name lifted daily to the altar of God. There is no condemnation in them. They are there to help you in a closer walk with the Lord. They are called! Those are the pastors that we need to search for. Those are the ones who love the Lord enough to love every soul they encounter.

Being a pastor is not a career that one should choose because of money, fame, or adulation. It should only be chosen if the God is calling you to it. Being a pastor is difficult and demanding work. In earlier times, the church did not support the pastor. They gave him donations at times but the tithes given to the Church were used for the upkeep of the church, for the poor and the needy. The pastors worked at other jobs to earn a living for their families. I still meet pastors who work a full-time job in addition to pastoring their church. If the church is large enough to support a pastor, full-time, then I see nothing wrong with giving the pastor a salary and benefits. If the church is needy, with many poor among them, then I think the pastor needs to find another way to earn an income. Remember that our tithes are given to God, not to a single person.

Summary and Reflection

Reflect on why you are at a particular church.

Is it because God placed you there, or are you attending because that's where your friends and people you want to know are?

If you see a problem at your church, have you prayed and received a clear answer from the Lord on how to address it? Have you fasted and asked the Lord for a clear answer? If you have and you feel led by the Lord, go to the pastor first, without condemnation. Talk the problem over with him/her. Make sure that this is not something only you are thinking or guessing at. If the pastor refuses to hear what you have to say, go back into prayer and fasting, and be sure to wait upon the Lord for clear direction.

If the problem is still not addressed or solved, go to the elders, in humbleness. If they refuse to listen, then maybe God wants you somewhere else. Don't leave and badmouth the pastor or church, though. Pray for them. Fast for them until God gives you a release. When you leave, leave in love, not anger.

And he gave some, apostles; and some, prophets; and some, evangelists; and some pastors and teachers; for the perfecting of the saints, for the work of the ministry, for the edifying of the body of Christ (Ephesians 4:11-12).

Notice that He did not say that whoever wants to go into the field of being a pastor, a shepherd of the flock, is called by Him. The scripture says He gave some as pastors and teachers.

Chapter 23
By His Leading

Often I have visions and dreams. I do not believe in psychics or those who speak with the dead. The Word says, *We are confident, I say and willing rather to be absent from the body, and to be present with the Lord.* (2 Corinthians 5:8) The Word doesn't say that we hang around and disturb God's children. The Word also says there is a great chasm between earth and heaven that no living man can cross.

But *I do* believe in dreams and visions from the Lord. I cannot cause them to happen at will and never know when they are going to happen. I might be speaking with someone, and the Lord will show me something from the person's life. It is *always* for the betterment of the person and to bring them closer to the Lord. There are times I have even had a vision or dream that has saved my life or the life of another.

I also have dreams occasionally and hear the same male voice in my dreams. The voice will tell me not to forget the dream or will direct me to tell someone something. I began having these dreams as a child and I was afraid of them. When I would tell my parents, they would urge me not to tell anyone, although my dreams and visions always came to pass. It wasn't until my son went into a coma that I prayed about it and decided I better begin listening to the Lord. Again, I did not feel worthy enough to believe God would tell me anything, but God has permitted me to see and hear because I get silent and listen.

In the Old Testament, God used a donkey to talk to man. I guess if He could use a donkey (Numbers 22:30), He could use me. I have wished that I could have a vision from God when *I* wanted to, but I have repented before the Lord.

Life-and-Death Obedience

My son had been ill for about a month. He had been putting on tremendous amounts of weight and yet all he was eating was fruit and he was buying it by the box. I told him he had to see a doctor or his father and I were going to drag him to one. I was praying, but my spirit was not settling. He finally saw a doctor on a Friday afternoon. During his office visit he "fell asleep" on her examining table and she had a difficult time waking him. She did check his blood sugar and told him he "might" have diabetes, gave him a prescription, and sent him home.

He telephoned us when he arrived home and said he was so tired he was barely able to drive. His dad and I went to see him. My spirit would not calm down. (Of course, I wasn't being quiet and listening, either. The mother part of me was panicking!)

He didn't look "right" and was still eating only fruit. He kept falling asleep while talking with us, and we told him he needed to go to the emergency room. He said the doctor told him to take the medication and he would be fine. What he and his dad and I didn't know was that his blood sugar topped her scale. It had registered as far up as her office scale could go. I knew nothing about diabetes at that time. He said we shouldn't worry and just go home.

My husband said "Let's go and let him sleep. Maybe he'll feel better after some rest." My husband told him we would telephone him every hour or so and he said okay. I could tell that my husband wasn't feeling right about our son, either, and all I could do at that time was remain in a state of panic for my child. I kept trying to stand on the Word, but I was too into my own flesh.

We went home, and Sanford and I prayed all evening in between telephone calls to our son. We both fell asleep quite late from pure exhaustion, and the second I fell asleep (I was finally putting my human mind aside and able to hear the Holy Spirit through my spirit) I saw my son lying dead! I awoke with a start and heard a voice say, "Go to him." It was easy to rebuke these thoughts, voices, and images since I believed they were from the devil. Even though throughout my life, these visions always came to pass, I continued to rebuke them.

I was terrified of the devil using me as a psychic. If the devil could use me in that way, it meant to me that I was never saved and unworthy of being saved. I would not permit my mind to entertain those thoughts. I kept my human mouth going as fast as I could. I kept rebuking the devil and claiming the blood of Jesus and repeating Jesus' name over and over and over until I just collapsed. I woke in the morning with a startle, knowing my son was dead. My husband woke at the same time and telephoned our son. There was no answer. He telephoned again and again. No answer. He told me to get my coat on because we were going to our son's house.

"No!" I said, "You go, I'll wait here." I could not go and bear to see my son, whom I loved with all my heart, dead.

My husband raised his voice and said "Get up, you are going!"

Almost paralyzed with fear for what we would find, I went with him. Sanford used his key and we found the house quiet. As we went down the hall toward the bedroom we called his name, there was no answer.

We walked into the bedroom and rushed to our son. Michael was already turning blue. Both of us tried to shake him awake while literally screaming his name. I dialed 911 and called for an ambulance. I never gave them an address or name but the second I hung up, they were at the bedroom door. (Someone told me to change the last sentence to "it seemed like the second I hung the phone up." But the truth is it was the second I hung the phone up. God performed a miracle.)

They both looked at our son and forced us to leave the room. They closed the door as we both heard one say to the other, "He's gone." Suddenly there were police there and so many people. I still don't know who they all were. They placed our son on a stretcher and tried to resuscitate him as they were taking him out. My husband told me to follow the ambulance with the car and he would go with our son.

I don't know how I drove to the hospital. I do not remember parking or walking. All I remember was walking into the emergency room and a nurse saying they were going to give him an intravenous injection of a very large tube of something. They were attempting to shock his heart. The nurse gave him one injection and looked at his father and me and said, "I have never had to give anyone two of these and had them live." He was still blue but his heart began to beat, slowly, but it beat. Then it would stop and it would beat.

I screamed my prayers out to the Lord and no one attempted to stop or quiet me. I knew then it was not the devil who told me to go to my son during the night; it was the Lord! I vowed then that I would never ignore His voice or visions again. I would never again believe that it was satan. I begged forgiveness and asked God not to hold my child responsible for my sins.

For the first time, I completely and totally gave my son to God. I was terrified, but I knew that God would complete His ultimate purpose and I would have to accept it no matter what. Eventually, they put Michael on life support. There were so many machines, needles, tubes, and monitors hooked to my baby lying on that table. All I could think was, "I did not give birth to you for this."

The team of doctors wanted to talk to his dad, his sisters, and me. The only thing I can remember their saying was that he probably would not make it through the night and suggested taking life support off of him. I looked at the doctor and said in a voice that was not even my own, "You are saying he will die, but my God did not tell me that. God and you will save his life."

While we were talking with the physicians, they had moved our son to ICU. The doctor took us to him and I was shocked to see that he was on even more life support equipment. I didn't think it possible. They told us the machines were causing his heart to beat, his kidneys to work, his blood to flow, and forcing oxygen into his lungs. There were tubes running from his leg to his heart. There were things I had never seen causing the blood to flow in his feet. The doctors told us that his blood sugars were over 2000, his cholesterol was 3000 plus.

I had never studied diabetes so could not understand any of it. All I knew was that I hoped, with every fiber of my being, that my son would live.

He was in a coma for 31 days. Almost every day, the doctors would tell us that he probably wouldn't make it through that day. Every day, I and my family said to them, "God did not tell us that." I'm sure they thought we were hysterical or needed to be medicated.

Sanford stayed with Michael day and night. He would not leave his side. I would go home and shower, sleep a little, and return. I was afraid to leave and afraid to stay. That human part that is fear kept popping up, even though I knew God would take care of him. I demanded a television in his room and put it on the cartoon channel. My son still loves cartoons. I would leave the room to get a cup of coffee or something to eat and come back to find one of the nurses had put the television on a soap opera channel. I would immediately change it back to cartoons for him.

On the thirtieth day, Michael began to come out of the coma. We were elated and praising the Lord! He began slowly by flickering his eyes. He still didn't understand us, but we were excited that the miracle had already happened. The doctors warned us that he probably had suffered some disabling effects, but they didn't know what kind of disabilities he would have or even if he would completely recover. Within two days he was awake. He wasn't speaking because of all the machines and equipment, but he would nod his head or move his finger to answer us. Slowly, he began to get better.

He had a bedsore on the back of his head that has caused a bald spot about the size of a quarter, which still upsets him. He had another bedsore on his back that took time to heal, but he is whole. There are no disabilities! It took time for him to come back to himself, but he has. The one major change that he experienced was a shift in values.

Prior to the coma, his only concern was how much money he could make, and he was making a lot. The material things he could purchase were of primary importance. Since then, money has not been as important. He let his business go to his partner; he sold his home and is a hardworking, good man. He still struggles with being a diabetic—but all diabetics, including me, have that struggle.

As I was writing this part about Michael, a strange thing took place. I began reliving it and my heart was breaking once again. I shed many tears writing this passage. Another strange thing happened. My youngest daughter and said something which I believe was a revelation from the Lord. She is very professional and usually is not emotional, but she said, "So, in my brother's attempt to hold onto his pride and dignity, he totally lost all of his pride and dignity."

What are you missing out on by not listening to His leading? Is it your health? Is it a deeper relationship with someone you really care about?

How often have I failed to do something out of fear of losing my own pride or dignity? I need to exercise and considered joining a fitness center, but because of my own pride, I did not want others to see me exercising, and heaven forbid that they should see me in exercise apparel. Everyone who looks at me realizes that I am a round person, although not as round as I once was. Do I think that if I clothe myself in certain garments it will make me look differently? Crazy thinking, isn't it? Yet I do it! I feel that I must maintain some dignity.

As I wrote this last sentence, it caused me to chuckle because that is something that I occasionally say: I must maintain some dignity. How foolish we are at times. Instead of donning some workout clothes and getting myself healthier, I sit in what I think hides my chubbies and I continue in my state of unhealthiness. (In writing this, I have made the decision to begin working out and becoming healthy.)

We all try to maintain our dignity and pride in different areas. Some of us are afraid of letting ourselves go in matters of the heart. We would never consider telling another how we truly feel, and often we die and never utter the words our loved ones are hungry to hear. We are afraid of appearing foolish.

Many of us are afraid to proclaim the Gospel of Jesus Christ to unbelievers, especially to those within our circle of friends. Most of us are afraid to even tell those we work with that we are Christians. We're afraid they might treat us differently or try to ignore us by not gossiping with us or telling dirty jokes around us. Praise the Lord! We're afraid that we won't be able to act the way we normally do around them. (Perhaps we are the bearers of gossip, or we're the ones telling the dirty jokes.)

Do we stop after work with co-workers to have a drink before heading home to our families? Do we gripe about our bosses or jobs, or swear at work? We would be better off proclaiming that we are Christians and then begin living it. It would make the world a better place to be in for all.

Is all we do in secret and before others, by His leading?

Summary and Reflection

If you have ever consulted a psychic, go to the Lord and ask forgiveness with a humble heart. He will forgive you. Ask Him to lead you and for only Him to lead you. Tell the Lord that you do not want to hear other voices, human or not, only His. He is a loving Father who will always lead His children in His way.

Have you ever consulted a psychic or one who believes they can speak with the dead? Please read all of Luke 16. In the chapter, Abraham speaks to a rich man who died and comes to ask Abraham to send someone to him in hell to dip his finger in cool water to take the pain from his tongue. Abraham tells him that there is a great gulf between heaven and earth which cannot be passed.

Please also read Luke 16:19-26, it also tells us that we cannot pass from heaven back to earth.

For the living know that they shall die: but the dead know not anything, neither have they any more of a reward; for the memory of them is forgotten (Ecclesiastes 9:5).

Whatever God tells you, He will confirm with His Word and with His dedicated children. True Christians will tell you God's truth and not tickle your ears attempting to please you or manipulate you.

Chapter 24
Miracles

I have been on a most exciting journey with the Lord this morning!

In 1970 and 1971, I had a total hysterectomy accomplished between two surgeries. Anyway, I was driving to work one morning sometime in August when I heard that gentle voice of the Lord speak and say "Go for a physical before there is cancer." I thought, "Hmm. Maybe this is something I should think about."

So, I did just that! I thought and pondered and I thought. I didn't want to rush into anything. I wondered if it was just my own mind thinking negative things.

The first of October, 2005, I woke up in the morning and was bleeding quite a bit. I immediately wondered where this issue of blood was coming from. I had nothing left to bleed from.

Then I stopped pondering and began acting. I was terrified!

Why hadn't I listened when I knew the Lord had spoken to me?

I called my doctor, and she gave me the first appointment of the day. When she checked me, she couldn't figure out where the blood was coming from, even though she saw the evidence. She ordered me to see a gynecologist immediately. You would have to know my physician, a beautiful woman from Jamaica who can really get tough when she's scolding a patient. She's also a faithful Christian, and I love her dearly. She made an appointment for me on the following day.

I was terrified of gynecologists and had not seen one for at least ten years. My doctor knew that I would never agree to see a male doctor, and we even discussed it again that day in her office. She just said "okay" and made me an appointment with a doctor. I assumed it was a female doctor, but when I got there, I was surprised that "he" was definitely not female.

I have to say that he is the nicest doctor, a Christian, and I'm so glad that God arranged for her not to tell me in advance that he was male. He was kind, considerate, and respected my modesty. We discussed the Lord and my work with HIV and those with mental health issues. I was hardly embarrassed at all. He found some areas that didn't look good and did surgery. The laboratory report came back less than a week later and the results were not good. They had found some cancerous cells. He had to do more surgery to be sure that he removed all of the cancerous cells. He scheduled the appointment for the beginning of February to wait for a complete healing, so he could see the areas he needed to remove while performing the surgery under a microscope.

I was a wreck. No faith! It was bad enough that I had to be examined and have surgery, but now he had to go back in again. I am a very modest person. Remember that God had told me in August to be checked? I was the one who didn't listen. I did not want anyone to examine me. Apparently, I believed God could and would take care of every area of my life except my modesty. I wanted control over that. Again, fear of losing my pride and dignity almost caused me to lose my life.

That morning, my youngest daughter called me and told me that she was coming before surgery to pray with me and to stay during the surgery. I didn't want her or anyone there besides my husband. I needed to be focusing on the Lord and getting myself together to endure the surgery without appearing like a baby girl. I seldom take pain medication unless absolutely necessary and will not permit anyone to put me to sleep. I have to remain focused on the Lord and not listen to anything else. But I was pleased to see my daughter and, yes, we prayed right in the waiting room, with no embarrassment. I hope it was a witness to everyone who was there.

When the doctor came in I told him, "No needles until you are sure what you're going to do." I told him that my grandson, my daughters, and my best friend had told me that God had taken care of it already, and that the doctor was going to be surprised when he found no cancer.

The doctor placed me in position for surgery and prepared what he needed. He then applied a solution and looked, applied more solution and looked, applied additional solution and looked. He asked his nurse to come and look. I was wondering what was going on. Finally, he said, "Caroline, the only thing I can see is healthy tissue."

I wanted to jump up and run out of there praising the Lord! I asked him if he was sure; I told him that my grandson Scott had taken my place at a healing service the previous Wednesday evening and told me I was healed. The doctor said there was nothing but healthy tissue, and I had healed perfectly! How excited I was! The doctor wanted to recheck me. Immediately, my stinking human thinking thought, "Next week, next month." But the doctor said. "in one year." I had to ask him to repeat it. I couldn't believe what he was saying. I believed God could do it, and I knew He could, but I was still shocked.

When I came out of there, my husband was looking at me with the biggest ear-to-ear smile I have ever seen. He knew! My daughter had gone to get breakfast, thinking it would take a while. I called my daughter's cell phone and she said "What? We'll be right there." When she arrived, she was praising the Lord with my husband and me. What a blessing the day had been! What a wonderful God we serve that He would look down on the likes of me and choose to heal me. Why? (Because if you were the only one, Jesus really would have laid His life down and died for just you.)

However, I will always remember my grandson standing in place for healing for his grandmother. I am so blessed! I know that God has always given me the grace to get through anything, even when "I" thought things were hopeless.

I have a dear friend, Lynn, undergoing breast surgery for a malignant tumor. Can God do the same for her? Of course, He can, but we never know His divine will. I later learned that she did have to endure surgery but the surgery was a success. She is cancer-free.

In my lifetime I have observed many miracles: my children being born, my grandsons, my husband, healings of family and friends. I have witnessed many miracles, too many to mention. Some of the most wonderful miracles I have experienced were accomplished by observing those addicted, those homeless, those starving coming to a saving knowledge of Jesus Christ and completely changing their lives. There are other miracles, bringing people, sisters and brothers from all ends of the earth to become my true brothers and sisters in Christ. Many have gone on to the Lord, but their friendship and love will always be miracles to me.

I remember one night when I was living in Oregon and sound asleep, when an angel of the Lord spoke to me in my dreams and ordered me to get to my knees and pray for the safety of my two daughters. I kept trying to go back to sleep, thinking it was foolish thoughts. The voice kept coming until I literally fell off the end of the bed onto my knees and began praying for their safety. As I was praying, the telephone on my nightstand rang and it was my youngest daughter calling. She was crying when I answered and said, "Mom, Sabrina and I just had a car accident." I asked if they were okay, and told her the Lord woke me up telling me to pray for them. They were both shocked, and so was I. The accident could have been much worse. There was only slight damage to both vehicles, and no one was injured. That was a miracle!

Have you ever witnessed or experienced something like that in your own life? If you have, write it down—it was a miracle.

Summary and Reflection

We all experience miracles. I do not believe there are any small miracles. A miracle is a miracle! Miracles are acts that only God can do.

Have you ever witnessed a miracle or miracles? Think back over your life and write them down. These are important to keep in your remembrance. They are the things to contemplate when you have those days and feel nothing good happens in your life. Go back and look at them when you feel that God isn't doing anything.

How great are His signs! And how mighty are His wonders! His kingdom is an everlasting kingdom and His domain is from generation to generation (Daniel 4:3).

And they went forth, and preached everywhere, the Lord working with them, and confirming the Word with signs following. Amen (Mark 16:20).

Ye men of Israel, hear these words; Jesus of Nazareth, a man approved of God among you by miracles and wonders and signs, which God did by Him in the midst of you, as ye yourselves also know (Acts 2:22).

Chapter 25
Death

There have been many times in my life that I have prayed for a healing for myself or another but have not seen a direct healing. I have wondered and thought; surely the healing would be for the good. It must be God's plan. God always answers, but sometimes His answer is to wait.

Often we have no idea what His plan is or even what the ultimate good is. I prayed for years for my mother's healing, but she passed on to glory. She was healed, but not in the way I desired. Her death was a healing for her. So death is not the end all, and death can and is a healing.

We cry and fret when our lives or the life of someone we love is threatened. It's because *we* will miss their presence. But they are just going on a trip. It would be the same if we had booked a trip to Hawaii or Tahiti or even Alaska. Many of us have never been to those places and don't know what to expect. Even though others who have been there tell us stories of the beauty, we really do not realize it until we see it for ourselves.

None of us would be afraid to travel to a destination that we've always dreamt of and heard wonderful things about. We believe those places are there because others have related it to us. It is the same with heaven. God told us about it. He's shared the beauty and peace in the Bible. We just haven't seen it or experienced it for ourselves. Humans will lie to us about what they've seen and witnessed, but God never will. What wonders await us!

A few days following the miracle I talked about in the previous chapter, I was watching our local news station. A young girl about fifteen years old was telling about her large brain tumor. She had been in the hospital awaiting surgery in the morning, but the night before, she fell on her knees before the Lord and prayed all night.

Out of her hospital room and in the night sky she saw a large ball of light. She stared at it all night while she was praying. It slowly became smaller and smaller until it totally disappeared. In the morning when the doctors did a scan on her brain prior to the surgery, the tumor was completely gone. Praise our precious Lord! She was healed!

The ball of light that she witnessed had to be a miracle from God, and she was praising the Lord on television. She said she knows God has a purpose for her and she would live the rest of her life for the Lord. What a witness her testimony was to me—and, I'm sure, to thousands of people.

God doesn't always choose to heal us in a conventional way. Sometimes He chooses to bring us Home to Him. Death isn't the end of life; it is the beginning of a new and better life. A life with the Lord. One where you can share with Him and be in His presence like you have never experienced before. In our human life, we can only imagine what it will be like to be able to walk with the Lord and talk to Him. Even though death can be a scary thought to many people, it is also the beginning of eternity with our Lord and Savior.

We mourn the passing of our loved ones and friends. However, we also need to remember it isn't the end and to celebrate that they are finally Home. A Home where there is no more suffering, no more trials, no more hurt, no more war, and no more death. Only life and His all-encompassing love and fellowship.

Summary and Reflection

Verily, verily, I say unto you, He that heareth my word, and believeth on Him that sent me hath everlasting life, and shall not come into condemnation; but is passed from death unto life (John 5:24).

Do you really believe what you proclaim to believe? The Word says that we do not pass from life to death, but that we pass from death to life.

We know that we have passed from death unto life, because we love the brethren. He that loveth not his brother abideth in death (1 John 3:14).

There are people who don't know what it is to really live. Are you one of them? Do you believe what the Lord said about passing to heaven? Contemplate your fears of death, and then take it to the Lord and ask Him to heal those fears. If you believe one word He said, you have to believe all of what He said.

Then shall the dust return to the earth as it was: and the spirit shall return unto God who gave it (Ecclesiastes 12:7).

Do you know when you pass in the twinkling of the eye you will be in heaven. Your spirit will never die, never grow old, never become ill and never shed a tear. God will make you new.

For me to live is Christ, and to die is gain. But if I live in the flesh, this is the fruit of my labour; yet what I shall choose I wot not. For I am in a strait betwixt two, having a desire to depart, and to be with Christ; which is far better (Philippians 1:21-23).

We are often conflicted. We want to be with our Lord and Savior in heaven, but at the same time we are afraid of the transition from our human bodies to our heavenly bodies, which will be eternal. This is natural and we need to pray and ask the Lord to deliver us from this fear.

Therefore we are always confident, knowing that, whilst we are at home in the body, we are absent from the Lord: For we walk by faith, not sight: We are confident, I say, and willing rather to be absent from the body, and to be present with the Lord. Wherefore we labour, that, whether present or absent, we may be accepted of him (2 Corinthians 5:6-9).

If you have accepted the Lord in your heart and professed with your mouth that He is Lord, then you will be accepted by Him.

Chapter 26
Surrender

We all are born with a mission that God has uniquely planned just for us. His designs and plans are beyond our thinking. When I was young, I always believed that I had no purpose other than to cause trouble and to be in trouble. I truly believed that was my sole purpose. I was no good for anything else. There were no gifts that I was given. A joke everyone told went, "When God asked if you wanted brains, you thought He asked if you wanted trains and said you would pass on that one." I really thought that was me.

When I accepted the Lord's gift of salvation at twenty-seven years old, my life began to change. Since my salvation, I have always done something to help others or to make their lives easier. Sometimes it was nothing more than accepting them as they were. Often it meant going to someone's home and helping them clean or do laundry. Sometimes it meant purchasing food and placing it at their door and leaving, or paying a bill for them without anyone's knowledge. I never realized that what I was doing was a gift from the Lord.

When I began studying the Bible and went to Bible College classes, the pastor asked what our gifts were. I couldn't answer because I didn't believe I had any. I would go out on the streets and as the Lord led me, I would give what I had to those who had nothing.

The Coat
My daughter recently brought up an instance that I had long forgotten.

I had seen a beautiful acrylic fur coat that I wanted so bad that I coveted it. Finally, the Lord permitted me to have the funds to purchase it when it went on sale. I loved that coat. It made me feel warm and beautiful when I wore it. But I did not even have it a week when I saw a poor woman living on the street who had nothing. I stopped and prayed with her and began to go on my way when I clearly heard the Lord speak to me.

He said, "Give her your coat."

I almost choked. I knew I had not heard the Lord correctly. I started to walk on and I heard His voice again. But I also heard in my heart that I had never asked God if He wanted me to have that coat. My sin was coveting that coat. I had placed that beautiful coat before God. I was not willing to give it up.

As I walked back to that poor woman with the coat in my hand, I covered her shoulders and she said, "Oh my God, thank you, God." She was not thanking me. She was thanking the One who always knew that coat was for her. She had her priorities right! She did thank me after she thanked God. I told her that the coat was never meant for me but was meant for her. I told her to praise God for it, but she was far ahead of me in praising Him from the moment it went on her shoulders. Funny that she was the same size as me. She went on her way, snuggly warm in that beautiful coat, and she looked like an angel in it.

Not many people ever knew that story. My ex-husband was very angry with me when I told him I had given the coat away. He told me that I had no consideration for money and that I was wasteful. But our precious Lord had taught me a lesson that was priceless. I do not believe that I have coveted anything since then. There have been times when I have almost slipped, but I always remember that lesson.

Does that mean that God does not want us to have beautiful things? No, certainly not. He wants the best for

His children. But God also wants our hearts right with Him. We are to covet nothing. We, as Christians, should always be ready to give, not of our abundance but from our need, and always our best for Him and His purposes.

When my daughter reminded me of the coat, she told how she and others thought I was crazy at the time. She knew I was doing it for the Lord, but she also knew how badly I had wanted (coveted, sin is sin) that coat. She said it didn't really make sense to her then, but it makes perfect sense now that she has given her life to the Lord.

To tell the truth, she is the same way. She would give anything if the Lord asked her to. Sometimes he asks us to give items away, sometimes he tells us to give away intangible things.

Have you had God ask you to give something up? It can be really hard.

Has God ever told you to give some ONE up? That is far more painful, isn't it? Surrendering relationships to God can be very difficult, but God still asks our obedience.

My daughter was in love with a man of God. I have seen and heard her tears over this man, without his ever knowing. The thing that amazed me in her was when she said to me "Mom, if it's God's will that he be with someone else and not with me, I will support him and pray for him no matter what." She said he was a good and Godly man whether he was with her or not.

I thought of how God was still performing astonishing miracles from that coat. It was breaking my heart when I realized God wanted me to give that coat away, but my daughter's heart was truly breaking when she was willing to give the man she loved, with all her heart, to the Lord.

She knew that this was the one God had intended for her from time beginning, and yet all she wanted was God's perfect will and this man's life to be led by the Lord.

She was such a witness to me when she shared that. How can I ever compare with what she has done?

I gave a coat—which, this many years later, would have been in rags and probably at the bottom of the trash heap. She was willing to give something that would last a lifetime in her heart, her spirit, and her emotions.

Summary and Reflection

Is there anything the Lord is asking you to surrender or give up?

But I would not have you to be ignorant, brethren, concerning them which are asleep, that ye sorrow not, even as others which have no hope. For if we believe that Jesus died and rose again, even so them also which sleep in Jesus will God bring with Him. For this we say unto you by the word of the Lord, that we which are alive and remain unto the coming of the Lord shall not prevent them which are asleep. For the Lord Himself shall descend from Heaven with a shout, with the voice of the Archangel, and with the trump of God: and the dead in Christ shall rise first: then we which are alive and remain shall be caught up together with them in the clouds, to meet the Lord in the air: and so shall we ever be with the Lord. Wherefore comfort one another with these words. (1 Thessalonians 4:13-18).

Every one of us needs to be witnessing. Are you afraid to talk to strangers? Are you afraid they will scoff at you? They scoffed at Jesus Christ, and they may at you. If you are afraid, take a trusted Christian brother or sister with you. Never go alone unless you know that the Lord is truly leading you. What He ordains He will bless and protect.

Often our best witness is the way we live our lives. How do you witness to those within your family? Do they count, or are you continually angry and snappy with them? Often it is easier and more comfortable to witness to a stranger than it is to a family member or friend. Family and friends know us too well.

For all have sinned, and come short of the glory of God; being justified freely through the redemption that is in Christ Jesus: whom God hath set forth to be a propitiation through faith in His blood, to declare His righteousness for the remission of sins that are past, through forbearance of God (Romans 3:23-25).

When you are witnessing to others who don't know Jesus Christ or are not living a Godly life, remember the scripture above.

Chapter 27
The Love of God

Last night about 10 P.M., my husband and I were getting ready for bed. He let our thirteen-year-old Pomeranian out for the last time of the evening, and I was turning the heat down for the night, when I heard him call me. He said, "You need to come and look at Snuggles. She is choking!" By his tone I knew this was not going to be a good thing. "No, I don't want to look." I knew that if I looked, it was going to be bad and I could not face anything happening to my little Snuggles. I really love her.

Over the years, she has become a true family member. When my son came out of the coma and stayed with us, Snuggles would lie on his chest the entire day and night and just stare into his eyes. She was taking care of him, and we would have to force her to go out to eat and drink. She was totally devoted to him for over two weeks. When our grandsons, Scott and Micah have stayed with us when they were ill, she maintains a watch in their bedroom. When our daughter, DeAnna, stayed with us during a terrible bout with the flu, Snuggles set watch. She does not leave their side.

After frantic telephone calls to our veterinarians and getting a message that the closest open vet was about twenty miles away, we drive 75 miles an hour down a 55-mile-an-hour windy road, with a choking dog. After x-rays the veterinarian informed us that the raw hide chew I had bought for her as a treat was stuck in her intestines. Thank God, the vet, along with the Lord, saved our little girl. They aren't permitting us to pick her up until late this afternoon, a fact that we are not happy about, but she's been on oxygen, had breathing treatments, and many other things in the interim. We are devoted to this dog because she has been devoted to each of the seven of us for thirteen years.

Today, while pondering last night's events, I was thinking how much Snuggles reminds me of the ways our precious Lord watches over us and how much He loves us. I am not daring enough to even hint that an animal would love and care for us as much as God does, but Snuggles sure displays the love more deeply than we humans do.

I considered her "watch" and thought about how that is exactly how God watches over us. He said He will never leave us or forsake us. He chose to give His very life for us. When we are hurting, God does all that He can to heal our hurts. His only desire is that we are healed and that we walk with Him. He loves us so much that His only desire is to share His heavenly home with us for eternity.

I have observed Snuggles when my husband or one of our children or grandchildren leave a room or leave the house. Suddenly her little ears will stand straight up, at attention, and she wants to know where we are and what we're doing. Sometimes it's only because she afraid she's missing out on a snack, but, nevertheless, she has to find us. When we leave the house, she barks and barks and even cries at times. Wow! What unadulterated love and devotion. God has an even greater love and devotion that we cannot begin to comprehend.

I hate to admit it, but often I take Snuggles for granted. I'm busy, I'm rushed, I'm tired, my attention is diverted to something more important and she is ignored. But, the second I call her name or even look in her direction, she runs to me and wants only to love me. God is that way, only so much better.

We ignore Him.

We don't take the time to talk with Him, and worse, we don't bother to hear Him speak to us.

We don't want to get up early for church and certainly don't want the service to last too long.

We don't want to volunteer for anything that might bring the unsaved to Him. We're busy! We're busy with the life that He alone gave us; we're busy with the jobs that He blessed us with; friends, family, cooking, cleaning, television, novels, running, social activities take our time and then we are just too darned tired to spend any time, much less quality time, with Him.

Yet, He is there! He is totally devoted, totally loving and forgiving. All we have to do is ask Him to forgive us, and He does! As much as I love the Lord, I still cannot comprehend that unselfishness. I get irritated when clients or friends take too much of my time. When demands are placed on me, I'm not always willing to greet them with a smile. I want to be away! I need my solitude. I need rest.

But He's not like that. What an amazing God we serve!

As soon as I wrote this last sentence, I was convicted. Are we "serving" God or are we looking for Him to serve us? I believe if we truly admitted our fault and our selfishness, we would say the majority of the Church is looking for Him to serve us. What a sad commentary on our lives. I stand ashamed.

My husband and I are so excited about picking Snuggles up this afternoon, and we've gone through the house making sure there's nothing she could choke on. We've thrown away anything made from rawhide or animal hides. We've checked the yard and the carpeting. We have her food ready and fresh, cool water standing by. We will fuss over her and hug her and just continue petting her and cooing to her.

But how long will it be before we forget last night's trial? We are human, and because we are, we will shortly begin to take her for granted again until the next emergency.

We do that with God, too. When we are in trouble or need healing, we are on our knees, gushing out prayers and asking forgiveness for everything we can think of. We even pull up sins we never committed to cover all bases. Then time passes, and we again take Him for granted.

He's the God of the Universe, the all-knowing, all-seeing God. Won't He always be there? Of course, He will, but will we? No! Our time is short on this earth. We are designated a certain time, and that is all we have. We each have a mission He gave us to fulfill while we are here.

Have we fulfilled His request? Don't think that if we fail, God will not use someone else. He will use whomever He can to have His purpose fulfilled. We can refuse and walk away, but God will use the one who is willing. How tragic it will be to meet Him in heaven and not have Him say, "Well done, my good and faithful servant." I cannot fathom the shame.

As a child of God, I desperately want Him to say to me, "Well done, my good and faithful servant." So, what do I have to do? *I have to be willing. Simply willing.*

That does not mean that I have to give away everything I have and wear sackcloth and ashes. If He asked me to, I want to be willing, but He has not asked that of me. He has asked me to go to the highways and byways and find His other children whom He loves so dearly and give them hope.

That hope is in the risen Christ! Our Savior, Jesus Christ, is the only hope any of us will ever have. He alone hung on the Cross. He alone took our sins on Himself so that when the Father looks at us, He sees only the spotless Blood of the Risen Lamb! When we ask forgiveness, the Father no longer sees our sins. He can see only the pure and wonderful gift that His Son, Jesus Christ, gave back to Him and to the world.

Sanford and I went to the vet and picked up our Snuggles. We were elated to see her, but it hurts my heart to see her little eyes showing she is not feeling well (her eyes show all her emotions) and acting as though she were afraid she had done something wrong. It's almost as though she's thinking, "What did I do that made them abandon me with strangers?"

She doesn't understand that we must do what we have to do in order to save her life. She doesn't understand that it's because we love her so much, and that we would do anything to help her feel better.

It's like that with God. Sometimes, we have events or other things happen in our lives and we cannot understand how a loving God would permit these things in our lives. We wonder what we have done wrong to cause Him to turn His back on us. We wonder why He seemingly no longer cares. All along, He is doing only what He has to do to save us for eternity. God will do all that is in His power to save us. That's why He created heaven. He didn't want to live there alone. He sent His Son, Jesus Christ, to this sin-filled earth to rescue us. He wants each one of us with Him in heaven.

He wants to spend all of eternity enjoying us and having us enjoy Him. I often try to imagine what His love must be like and I can't. I love my children and grandchildren with everything that I am capable of, but my love for them is nothing compared to His love for us. I would give my very life to save them, and yet it still wouldn't be near what Jesus gave when He gave His life. He was totally separated from the Father for a period of time. Our sins did that to Him, He knew, and yet was willing to undergo it.

Have you ever imagined what it would be like to be completely separated from God? We have not ever experienced it. No matter what our sin is or has been, God is still there waiting with open arms and forgiveness. It makes no difference if we are believers or unbelievers. We still have Him. But, to be separated I cannot presume to understand. That's terrifying for me. I never want to be in that spot.

We can walk away, but God is always waiting for us to return.

There were times in my life when I walked away from God. I chose other things over Him. I even toyed with satanism at one time in my young life. It was popular at a certain time when I was looking for what I needed. But even then, God never once left me for a millionth of a second. I can remember hearing that still, small voice in my spirit, calling me back to Him. He protected me, no matter where I was and what I did. He had a purpose for my life.

At times when I was walking in the world, I would become scared and I would cry out to Him. He never failed me. Even though I said I wanted nothing to do with Him, He still never left me. I never went so far as to renounce God or Jesus Christ or the Holy Spirit, but I sure acted it out. And through it all, God loved me and wanted me. What an example God has set for our relationships. Can we ever compare with Him? No, never!

We put our family and friends on short leashes. We do not, under any circumstances, want them to ever betray us. Forgiveness can be hard to come by. But God is always right with us to forgive us and open His arms to us.

Sometimes I think to myself, "This is completely unbelievable! It is just too awesome! It is too loving!" And then I remember that this was the reason we were created! He created us to love us!

Often when people tell me they are atheists, I comment to them that they have so much more faith than I will ever have. They usually look at me strangely and say, "No. I do not have faith. I do not believe in God." I always reply, "But you must have more faith than me. If I did not believe that God was holding the planets and stars together, I would die of terror wondering when they were going to come crashing down on us."

I also tell them if I did not believe that there was an omnipresent, omnipotent God who loved us and was so willing to forgive us, I would probably just check out of life. What would be the sense in living? This is a pretty horrible place without a loving, forgiving God.

Think about the mess the world is in today. Recently the police arrested the BTK (bind, torture, and kill) murderer. He was a leader in his church, a Boy Scout leader, worked for the city, and yet killed ten people by binding, torturing, and killing them. He may have appeared as a leader in his church, but he was certainly not a Christian believer. The Word says: *And no marvel; for satan himself is transformed into an angel of light. Therefore it is no great thing if his ministers also be transformed as the ministers of righteousness; whose end shall be according to their works* (2 Corinthians 11:14-15).

Our world is filled with sin and depravation today. Many say that if God does not return for his people soon, He will have to dig up Sodom and Gomorrah and apologize to them. Everything that has been despised is now loved and even coveted. Rape, murder, indescribable sexual sin, abuse, neglect—whatever was hated is now loved. We are a people who believe we have a right to our sin, no matter the cost to anyone else and no matter the cost of hurting the very heart of God.

Looking for Fulfillment

I have done street outreach for so long that for a while I believed I had seen and heard everything. But in my current position, I do community outreach and am still amazed when eleven- and twelve-year-olds relate to me that they are regularly having sex. And it's not just sex. It seems that it becomes increasingly depraved. I listen to youth and adults speak of their intimate lives and wonder why they cannot get fulfilled.

Then I realize that there is no spiritual connection between people any longer. That is why they are seeking more depraved sex and higher highs to fill the void of emotional emptiness. They are not spiritually or emotionally connected to their partners. Their relationship, their union, was never ordained by God. They will have sex with anyone, and often with anything, in order to seek some satisfaction, yet they never find it. They go from partner to partner to partner seeking true ecstasy and never find it. They continue on and on, seeking the one or the ones who will finally bring it to them. That's why they continue in their depraved states and become even more depraved and begin mutilating, torturing, and killing others. They do not realize they have only to fall into God's loving arms. He will fulfill every need they have. He will direct their steps and bring them complete satisfaction. They will be filled with a joy that is overflowing and all-encompassing. He will give them more joy than they ever imagined.

Our Snuggles gave us unconditional love. Even when she didn't feel good, she was always there for us and watching over us. There were times I would walk through a room and my foot would accidentally hit her because I didn't see her. She never tried to bite or retaliate in any way. She just came back to me with love. How many times have we hurt the Lord, yet He is always waiting for us with love, with arms open wide. He is always ready to forgive and love us. He loves us unconditionally.

Summary and Reflection

He that dwelleth in the secret place of the most High shall abide under the shadow of the Almighty. I will say of the Lord, He is my refuge and my fortress: my God; in Him will I trust. Surely he shall deliver thee from the snare of the fowler, and from the noisome pestilence. He shall cover thee with his feathers, and under his wings shalt thou trust: his truth shall be thy shield and buckler. Thou shalt not be afraid for the terror by night; nor for the arrow that flieth by day; Nor for the pestilence that walketh in darkness; nor for the destruction that wasteth at noonday. A thousand shall fall at thy side, and ten thousand at thy right hand; but it shall not come nigh thee. Only with thine eyes shalt thou behold and see the reward of the wicked. Because thou hast made the Lord, which is my refuge, even the most High, thy habitation; There shall no evil befall thee, neither shall any plague come nigh thy dwelling. For he shall give his angels charge over thee, to keep thee in all thy ways. They shall bear thee up in their hands, lest though dash thy foot against a stone. Thou shalt tread upon the lion and adder: the young lion and the dragon shalt thou trample under feet. Because he hath set his love upon me, therefore will I deliver him: I will set him on high, because he hath known my name. He shall call upon me and I will answer him: I will be with him in trouble; I will deliver him, and honour him. With long life will I satisfy him, and shew him my salvation (Psalms 91).

Anytime you are feeling fear, claim Psalm 91. If the fear doesn't go away, perhaps God is trying to tell you that it is something He doesn't want you do. Or it may be a place He doesn't want you going to. Remember that God sends those He wants in certain areas, and He may be sending you elsewhere. Send you He will, but it may not be where you want it to be. It is always good to have a list of scriptures written out that you can claim anytime you need to.

Chapter 28
A Melting Pot of Beliefs

While having coffee this morning, I was reading a magazine article about spirituality in our world today. My favorite thing is to read while enjoying a hot cup of coffee on my day off.

The article extolled the benefits of a new group of believers called the "Nones." I had never heard of this group although we've all met them and been exposed to their beliefs.

Apparently this group, with numbers still rising, was upward of 30 million in 2001 and has grown steadily since. A composite faith, they are embracing of Judaism, Buddhism, Reiki, Kabala, Catholicism, Hinduism, Christianity, New Age, and whatever else can be thrown into the pot. It's a feel-good religion. Its members claim it is a new spiritual awakening that is taking over the planet. God is everywhere and in everything, so they do not have to follow a certain set of beliefs. They can worship when and where they choose, often in Christian denominational churches.

Of course, they attend only when they feel like it. The article said, "They believe wisdom that arises out of sharing faiths is more important than something handed down from a religious authority." They also claim it is a democratizing of wisdom. The conclusion of the article stated, "Whatever path they choose, more Americans seem to be engaged in a reinvigorated pursuit of spiritual growth away from a religion found only inside a steepled church on Sundays and toward an everyday, individualized faith." (David France, "Search for Meaning", *Ladies Home Journal*, February 2005)

Here's the scripture that went through my mind as I read the article.

Be it known unto you all, and to all the people of Israel, that by the name of Jesus Christ of Nazareth, whom ye crucified, whom God raised from the dead, even by him doth this man stand here before you whole. This is the stone which was set at naught of you builders, which is become the head of the corner. Neither is there salvation in any other; **for there is none other name under heaven given among men, whereby we must be saved** (Acts 4:10-12).

Have any of these people ever read the Word of God? Do they really believe that God meant nothing He said in His Word? There is salvation in NO other! That is clear! No other can bring us what we are seeking. No other can bring us peace and sustenance. No other can bring us joy and forgiveness.

Who is a liar but he denieth that Jesus is the Christ? He is an antichrist that denieth the Father and the Son. Whosoever denieth the Son, the same hath not the Father: [but]he that acknowledgeth the Son hath the Father also. Let that therefore abide in you, which ye have heard from the beginning. If that which ye have heard from the beginning shall remain in you, ye also shall continue in the Son, and in the Father. These things have I written unto you concerning them that seduce you. But the anointing which ye have received of him abideth in you, and ye need not that any man teach you: but as the same anointing teacheth you of all things, and is truth, and is no lie, and even as it hast taught you, ye shall abide in him (1 John 2: 22-27).

The article tells us that the churches must come back out of the buildings and go to where the people are. I agree completely. But we also must realize that a place to meet and worship our Creator is necessary. Many desire to come together in an attitude of worship and fellowship. It is necessary. I do not understand what people have against the traditional churches as a meeting place to hear and share the Word of our God.

We have coffeehouses all over the world now where people come together. They sit at tables and discuss whatever is of interest to them, yet we ridicule those who meet to share their like-mindedness of the Lord. We have clubs and civic organizations designed solely for those interested in certain subjects, such as the Moose Clubs and the Optimist Clubs and those designed for book readings. We have organizations designed for every subject imaginable. You can find a group no matter what your particular interest is, yet we have a problem with the Christian church.

If our belief is in the Word of God and His Son, Jesus Christ, why is there so much opposition surrounding it? Is the devil afraid because he knows we have the Truth? I'm sure he would like nothing better than to see every Christian church closed and torn down.

The devil knows the truth, and he is terrified of it. He knows God and he knows Jesus Christ and the Holy Spirit, and he would like nothing better than to have the world searching for meaning elsewhere. If he can create a movement to get us away from salvation, his purpose would be complete. He would like nothing better than to see all of us fall into the pits of hell with him for eternity. Do we believe we will find our search for meaning with him in hell? No, we will never find it apart from the gift of Jesus Christ. That would be eternal damnation. Without Him, there is no meaning and no purpose for life.

As a young child, I was raised in the Catholic Church and attended Catholic schools. I also attended Greek and Russian Orthodox churches. In my search for God, during my younger years, I attended Religious Science, Buddhist Temples, many far-Eastern religions, and even satanic meetings.

I did not know what I was searching for. I think that I, like many of that time, were searching for truth and individual power. We were all pretty mixed up in our beliefs. When I finally came to accept the Lord Jesus Christ as my personal Savior, it was like I knew this was where I should always have been. I knew this was where I belonged and I knew that I would never leave Him again. There is truth, peace, and evidence in accepting Him. You can feel it in your spirit and know it is right.

I instantly knew there is only one God, one Jesus Christ, one Holy Spirit and one Trinity. I knew deep within myself, in that searching spot that we all have. I didn't want power. I wanted peace and comfort within Him. I have not always lived a good Christian life, but I have never wavered in my beliefs from that day until now. I sinned, but I knew that I had a Savior to go to who would forgive me and cleanse me from my sins. I cannot believe in a melting pot of beliefs. There is only one God!

Summary and Reflection

There is one body, and one Spirit, even ye are called in one hope of your calling; one Lord, one faith, one baptism, one God and Father of all, who is above all, and through all, and in you all (Ephesians 4:4-6).

Have you ever been so close to someone that you couldn't imagine never seeing them again? Would you be lost without their caring, love, and devotion in your life? What kind of a friend are you? Do you give your friends and loved ones the same devotion, caring, and love that you seek from them? Do you give unconditionally, or do you put conditions on that love?

For there is one God, and one mediator between God and men, the man Christ Jesus; who gave Himself a ransom for all, to be testified in due time (1 Timothy 2:5-6).

And the scribe said unto him, Well, Master thou hast said the truth: for there is one God; and there is none other but He: and to love Him with all the heart, and with all the understanding, and with all the soul, and with all the strength, and to love his neighbor as himself, is more than all whole burnt offerings and sacrifices (Mark 12:32-33).

Have you ever considered how you would react if you were asked to give your life for a loved one, a friend, or even a stranger? How would you react? Would you pray and ask the Lord's leading? Then would you follow it?

Chapter 29
The Question of Sin

Many people say that the Christian church always talks about sin. Everyone is a sinner. They are quick to tell us how tired they are of hearing it and that they are not sinners. They're just people trying to live a good life.

They say that if God really exists then surely He knows we all fail at times. It's normal. The Word says, *If we confess our sins, He is faithful and just to forgive us our sins, and to cleanse us from all unrighteousness If we say that we have not sinned, we make Him a liar, and His word is not in us* (1 John 1:9-10).

That is all there is to it! Confess! Nothing more, nothing less! He didn't say that we have to crawl 15 miles on our knees over broken glass or stones. He did not say that we must beat ourselves and perform all kinds of rigorous penances. He simply said, "Confess." How much easier could it be?

He is not a vengeful God, looking to punish or harm us.

He does not seek justice served like we do.

He wants to forgive our sins.

God calls for mercy. Everyone has sinned and continues sinning! I used to say that I was God's chief sinner until I realized what an arrogant remark it was. Yes, I have been and still am a sinner, always have been, and always will be. I sure wish I wasn't, but the minute I think I've got this sin thing conquered, I end up thinking a nasty thought about someone, or vegetate in front of the television, or eat something I know I shouldn't be eating. I'm sure not proud of it, but I am not chief of anything. I'm not even worthy to be His lowliest sinner. I am simply a sinner saved by the grace of God and Blood of the Lamb. It is His doing. Not mine. I have done absolutely nothing to deserve forgiveness.

The one thing we must remember is that in confessing our sin and asking forgiveness, we are repenting before God. Repentance basically means "a turn around." Biblical repentance has a greater meaning. Repentance is turning away from sin to God in order to put yourself wholeheartedly in God's trust that He will keep you from sin.

Repentance is changing our attitude, recognizing and accepting true responsibility for what we have done, and deciding to turn away from sin completely and turn our will, our actions, our thoughts, and our very life over to God.

We cannot blame anyone else, even partially. It is our sin that matters. We are responsible for what we have done and cannot shift the blame, as Adam attempted with Eve. True repentance always requires a broken heart over the sin we have committed. A change of lifestyle and behavior is absolutely necessary for repentance to be genuine. If we sin, and we admit that we are guilty of sin, that alone is not repentance.

True repentance requires having remorse for grieving the heart of God. It is being sorry that we have broken His law. If we have truly repented, we will change our life of sin. It's becoming a changed person. If we previously were involved in gossip, sex, laziness, arrogance, even murder, we must surrender to God once again and totally change our life. We must see sin for what sin is. It is turning your back on the One who saved you. It is turning your back on the Savior.

True repentance is the only thing that can bring you back to a state of wholeness. If you are misled and think yourself above true repentance, the only thing awaiting you is destruction and a false sense of salvation.

Summary and Reflection

And thou shalt love the Lord thy God with all thy heart, and with all thy soul, and with all thy mind, and with all thy strength: this is the first commandment (Mark 12:30).

Awake to righteousness, and sin not; for some have not the knowledge of God: I speak this to your shame (1 Corinthians 15:34).

What shall we say then? Shall we continue in sin, that grace may abound? God forbid. How shall we, that are dead to sin, live any longer therein? Know ye not, that so many of us as were baptized into Jesus Christ were baptized into his death? Therefore we are buried with him by baptism into death: that like as Christ was raised up from the dead by the glory of the Father, even so we also should walk in newness of life. For if we have been planted together in the likeness of his death, we shall be also in the likeness of his resurrection: Knowing this, that our old man is crucified with him, that the body of sin might be destroyed, that henceforth we should not serve sin. For he that is dead is freed from sin (Romans 6:1-7).

Leaving sin behind is difficult even when you have accepted Jesus Christ as your Lord and Savior. Sin is something that has become comfortable. It's like putting on a comfy old sweater and wrapping it around us. But when that sweater falls apart, we eventually pick another and wear it until it becomes as comfortable as the old, discarded one.

It's the same with sin. Once we walk away from it and live in the precepts of God, it becomes comfortable, more comfortable than we could have imagined. It becomes something we never want to let go of.

Therefore if any man be in Christ, he is a new creature: old things are passed away; behold, all things have become new. And all things are of God, who hath

227

reconciled us to Himself by Jesus Christ, and hath given to us the ministry of reconciliation (1 Corinthians 5:17-18).

Chapter 30
Celebrate

A young friend recently sent me a quote by Marianne Williamson which caused me to sit up and take note.

Our deepest fear is not that we are inadequate. Our deepest fear is that we are powerful beyond measure. It is our light, not our darkness, that most frightens us. We ask ourselves, "Who am I to be brilliant, gorgeous, talented, and fabulous?" Actually who are you not to be? You are a child of God. Your playing small doesn't serve the world. There's nothing enlightened about shrinking so that other people won't feel insecure around you. You are born to make manifest the glory of God that is within you. It's not just in some of us, it's in everyone. And as we let our own light shine, we unconsciously give other people permission to do the same. As we're liberated from our own fear, our presence automatically liberates others.

I had read this quote from Marianne Williamson before, but it never made the impact it did this time. This time it came alive for me. Ms. Williamson was absolutely correct!

I am afraid, terrified that I am powerful beyond measure. I am a child of the living God, and nothing is impossible for me. I see from this present moment forward. I cannot view as God does, from eternity back to this moment. He can see what He originally designed me to be. His design was for a perfect, healthy, intelligent, lovable child of God to be brought into this sin-filled world. The world helped to cause feelings of inferiority in me, and I helped and even welcomed it all along the way. I bought into what others said and did. It never occurred to me that I could be something other than what was tagged onto me. If someone said it, it must be factual. I never trusted myself or trusted God within me. When God said to me to move forward, the devil convinced me it was my own thinking and that I would fall on my face trying.

The devil is so deceitful and conniving, always trying to take credit away from God and cause His kids to stumble. I *permitted* the devil to cause me to stumble, and it's time to put a stop to it. My playing small has never served the world. My manifesting the glory of God will serve God and the world.

I have wanted to pursue my doctorate but have been afraid of failing. My husband has told me that if I want to pursue it, go for it. I think, "I'm too old," "I'm too tired," "How can I do the work required while I'm still working my job?" I'm not sure where or when I'm going to continue, but now I "know" I will when and if it is ordained by my Father. I no longer have a fear of going on or pursuing anything that the Lord has laid on my heart.

Often I hear Christians ask "How do I know this is God's will?"

If God has laid it on your heart, and you've prayed, and that desire just won't go away, then try that path. Seek good Christian counsel. But even if the world tells you not to pursue a certain thing, and yet the desire continues as you pray and seek God, go for it!

I have been teased for being nomadic at times of my life. I was born in Illinois, moved to California, then onto Oregon where I lived for almost thirty years, onto Hawaii for five or six years, back to Oregon, then to Oklahoma, and now in North Carolina for these last eleven years. I must say that every step I took, every place I've moved, and everything I've done, was ordained by God to bring me to where I am now spiritually.

Was I afraid at times that I was on the wrong path? Of course, I was. But each and every step brought me closer to my Savior. At each and every intersection and every path, God had me witnessing and ministering to others. I would not be afraid today if He asked me to move anywhere on this planet. There are times when I think the beach in Tahiti or the mountains of Alaska sound very appealing, but God has really not placed that in my heart. Those are my dreams, not God's.

I must say, though, that I am happy. I am happy because I serve our God. I have always loved the hymn that goes, "And He walks with me, and He talks with me, and He tells me that I am His own." That has spoken volumes to me over the years. I feel Him with me. I hear His voice. I know that He alone ordains my steps. What a wonderful journey this has been and will continue to be. I am His own, and so can you be, too! Just one of God's Raggedy Kids!

Note: I have not capitalized satan's name anywhere in this book. It was not done in error. I simply do not believe that his name is worthy to be capitalized.

Conclusion

Earl Coleman, who will always be a dear and trusted friend and confidante, shared something with me several years ago. I believe that it must be included before there is an ending. *When we finally let go of our past, our past will let go of us.* (Italics inserted)

How we perpetuate our low self-esteem

1. By lack of faith, both in ourselves and in an ordered, beneficent and purposeful God. *But let him ask in faith, nothing wavering. For he that wavereth is like a wave of the sea driven with the wind and tossed. For let that man not think that he shall receive anything of the Lord* (James 1:6-7).

2. By lacking a sense of meaning and purpose in life and, thus, clear-cut goals and objectives to motivate and guide our decisions and endeavors. Thus we lack a sense of progress toward accomplishment. *And we know that all things work together for good to them that love God, to them who are the called according to His purpose* (Romans 8:28).

3. By depending on others for a sense of importance and realness. *According to the eternal purpose which he purposed in Christ Jesus our Lord: In whom we have boldness and access with confidence by the faith of him* (Ephesians 3: 11-12).

4. By failing to accept complete responsibility for our life and well-being. By not taking full charge of our own life and directing it into (God's) constructive channels. *And Jesus said unto her, Neither do I condemn thee; go, and sin no more* (John 8:11b).

5. By self-indulgence and doing what comes easiest. By reacting instead of thinking and acting for ourselves. *This is a faithful saying, and these things I will that thou affirm constantly, that they which*

have believed in God might be careful to maintain good works. These things are good and profitable unto men (Titus 3:8).

6. By failing to recognize and exercise our own innate authority (free will) to make our own decisions. By depending on others for what we can and need to do for ourselves. By requiring the permission, confirmation, and agreement of others. (*This is a good way to follow others' leading and not the Lord's.*)

7. By adhering to false concepts, values, and assumptions that engender condemnation, blame, and guilt and thus destroying any remaining vestige of self-esteem. *That we henceforth be no more children, tossed to and fro, and carried about with every wind of doctrine, by the sleight of men, and cunning craftiness, whereby they lie in wait to deceive* (Ephesians 4:14).

8. By identifying with our actions and not differentiating between who we ARE and what we DO. By indulging in self-blame, shame, guilt, and remorse. *For ye are bought with a price; therefore glorify God in your body; and in your spirit, which are God's* (1 Corinthians 6:20).

9. By failing to develop our inherent capabilities and talents in order to make the most of our innate God-given potential. *I can do all things through Christ which strengtheneth me* (Philippians 4:13).

10. By not allowing ourselves the right and freedom of full expression to make mistakes to goof off and to, yes, even fail. *If any of you lack wisdom, let him ask of God, that giveth all men liberally, and upbraideth not; and it shall be given him* (James 1:5).

11. By making comparisons with others a gauge of our own worth and by feeling we are required to "prove ourselves better than," not realizing that what

another does or does not do has no valid bearing on our own worth or importance. *For we are his workmanship, created in Christ Jesus unto good works, which God hath before ordained that we should walk in them* (Ephesians 2:10).

12. By neglecting to take any appropriate action within our capabilities, no matter how small or seemingly unimportant, that will enhance our sense of self-worth. *But let every man prove his own work, and then shall he have rejoicing in himself alone, and not in another* (Galatians 6:4).

13. By resisting or being fearful and anxious about things we can do nothing about, instead of facing up to and accepting the reality of what is. *Be careful (anxious) for nothing; but in every thing by prayer and supplication with thanksgiving let your requests be made known unto God. And the peace of God, which passeth all understanding, shall keep your hearts and mind through Christ Jesus* (Philippians 4:6-7).

14. By being impatient, harsh, and demanding with ourselves. *For God hath not given us the spirit of fear; but of power, and of love, and of a sound mind* (1 Timothy 1:7).

Epilogue

My son is doing well with his diabetes. He has learned through this disease that wealth and prestige do not bring happiness or serenity. He walks closely with the Creator and has a mission in life to help others. He is definitely an encourager and an uplifter. He is also one of my best friends. He has learned that eating according to God's laws and exercising are necessary. God knew what He was doing when He gave us our dietary laws. If the Creator said it, that's good enough for him.

Our eldest daughter is fulfilling her purpose. She knows that she has found her calling, and her self-esteem is where our precious Lord meant it to be all along. She now has a confidence in herself, with the Lord that I have always known was there. She is one of those people who can make you laugh until you hurt. She definitely has the gift of laughter, a precious gift. Sabrina says, "If God says it, I believe it, and that's final." She admits that she is like a child with Him.

Our youngest daughter is dedicated wholly to the Lord and her church. She will do anything the Lord asks of her. She studies the Word of God constantly and has so many notebooks where she has taken notes as she studies. Her time is spent giving to others and attending church. Wherever she is, from the auto mechanic to a total stranger, she will talk to them about the Lord and ask if they are reading their Bible, but never in a threatening way. She is loving them into the kingdom of God.

My husband is doing well and is a witness to me daily of what we can do, no matter our limitations. Several years ago, he was diagnosed with latent tuberculosis that he probably contracted while serving in the U.S. Navy. He continues to be active and has a positive outlook. As he tells everyone, "God is in control, not you and not me." He doesn't just say it, he lives it.

It is all in God's perfect will. He is a wonderful husband, father, and grandfather. He attempts to encourage everyone he meets to finish school if they have not, and to attend college and get a degree. He is my emotional support.

I suffered an accident with complications in the spring and am no longer employed. Of course, I'm always employed by the Lord. He can use me for His will anytime, anywhere, accident or not.

A Simple Prayer

Today,
For what I am that I ought not to be,
Forgive me.
For what I am not that I ought to be,
Forgive me.
Be with my mouth in what it speaks
Be with my hands in what they do
Be with my mind in what it thinks
Be with my heart in what it feels
Work in me
...through me
...for me
...in spite of me
In the precious name of Jesus,
Amen (author unknown)

About the Author

A "Nomad for God", Caroline Clark has lived all over the country. Born and raised in Chicago, Caroline has lived in Hawaii, where she was ordained, Oregon, Oklahoma, and now makes her home in North Carolina.

While trying to come off speed, marijuana, and alcohol, Caroline met Jesus at the age of 27. She completed high school at the age of 49, earning her GED in just 3 weeks after being told all her life she couldn't learn. She then earned a bachelor's in psychology and a Master's in Human Relations. She knows that whoever you are, whatever you've done, Jesus is waiting for you to come back to His arms. Stains and all.

You can find out more at:
www.theroadtoacceptance.com

www.ingramcontent.com/pod-product-compliance
Lightning Source LLC
LaVergne TN
LVHW092316080426
835509LV00034B/260